Prologue

Why should you read another memoir about me? Well, in this book you will read some additional stories about my careers and life after transitioning that you may find interesting, serious, funny, and possibly even cringe worthy. I have had many amazing things happen in my life that I want to share with you in the hopes you will take more risks in your life and reap the rewards that follow. I hope you enjoy reading "Foggy Googles."

FOGGY GOOGLES

A sequel memoir to

Do You Know Who Once Was?

Cami Richardson

Published in the United States by Kindle Direct Publishing

Library of Congress Cataloging-in-publication data is available upon request

ISBN: 9798436588681

eBook ISBN- N/A

Printed in the United States of America

Book cover design by Deb Browne

Edited by Alison Kae

First Addition

Other books by author: Do You Know Who I Once Was?

TABLE OF CONTENTS:

Dedication

I spent over 20 years of my life in love with an amazing spouse, partner, woman, mother, grandmother, daughter, sister, nurse, and friend to many. Her name is Lorraine Davies. People often say how courageous I am for coming out as trans. What was truly courageous was Lorraine fighting for her life for over 11 years with a brain tumor. She lost her battle in early 2021 and I felt a true sense of loss. I am so thankful that she gave me two beautiful daughters in Erin and Lindsay. Mostly, I am thankful that we always managed to respect each other despite our divorce. We never fought and our daughters saw that and admired it. I loved when I told her I was coming out as trans—as Cami— and she immediately accepted me, and that acceptance never faltered.

Lorraine, this book is dedicated to you. Thanks for everything. You made a difference in my life and many others.

"Foggy Googles" is a sequel memoir to my first book called "Do You Know Who I Once Was?" In my discussions with my editor on the first book, she suggested I leave out many of my stories and memories about my firehouse years, my amazing wife Teri, my ski career, and entrepreneurial years and try to focus the book on my transition to that of being a transgender woman. I agreed and I believe that first book helped me move forward in reaching my personal mission and goal of educating and enlightening others about the transgender community. After publishing it and in allowing some friends and family to read some chapters that were left out, the common response I received was that I should publish them and include them in a sequel, so "Foggy Googles" became a reality. This book will also include an update on my transition over the past six years, which have been some of the most rewarding of my life.

Why the name "Foggy Googles?" Well, in the book I speak of my 50 years of being a skier and having a career in the ski industry. If you know anything about skiing and have had an experience with having foggy googles while skiing, you realize that it can lead to crazy results. Your vision could be impaired, and many funny, sad, or unbelievable events could happen. In this book you will read about some of my personal stories, and I believe you will enjoy hearing some of my own "Foggy Goggles" experiences.

It was interesting for me to look back on my life and recall the good and the bad, the fear and the calmness, the excitement and the disappointments, the growth and the regressions, the sorrow and the love and the acceptance and rejection.

I am no different than most of you in how I have lived my life. I have taken on lots of risks in my life and careers and I am not afraid of sharing my experiences in the hopes that you can learn something and even have the courage to take on more risk and achieve more in your life. I hope in reading this book you will laugh, cry, enjoy it, but mostly, I hope you live your life to the fullest. Godspeed on your journey.

Cami

Foreword

How do two lifelong friends react when told by their mutual friend, Tom, that he is becoming she? What did it all mean? Were we going to lose our friend? We had shared many moments of our lives together, including being a part of Tom's wedding party. We worked with Tom for years in the ski industry and witnessed tenacity, leadership and collaboration to accomplish objectives, including building, and then naming, a restaurant/bar at Sunday River Ski Area in Maine, Foggy Goggles,

Foggy goggles can be a metaphor for life in many respects. It can be as literal as skiing when goggles fog up. That fog can cloud reality and create concern for what is ahead. Was this real? What does this mean? Surprised does not even come close to our initial reaction. We felt uncertain, much like having blurred vision. We traveled to Park City to spend time with Cami and her wife, Teri, shortly after the transition news was shared. We were concerned about how this change would affect them and their lives, and to see Cami first-hand as a transgender female. Teri's acceptance helped us move closer to feeling the same.

Since transitioning, Cami has embraced a new energy to help educate and engage others to be their authentic selves and to help people accept those who appear different. The same tenacity, courage, and leadership we saw in Tom continues as Cami has become a strong advocate for transgender people through interviews, lectures, and outreach programs to LGBTQ groups.

This is a story of one's remarkable journey to become her authentic self, while navigating a successful career in many endeavors. Our friendship remains strong, our goggles are clear. Do not judge a book by its cover but take the time to turn a few pages. This book is worth reading.

Brian Ganey
Scott Karn

Growing Up

I grew up in Poughkeepsie, New York, which was best known for being one of IBM Corporation's largest manufacturing plants in the world, as well as the famous lines by Gene Hackman in The French Connection ("I'm gonna nail you for picking your feet in Poughkeepsie") and Carrie Bradshaw in the Sex and the City movie ("Charlotte Poughkeepsied in her pants"). So, maybe not so famous.

At its peak in the '50's, '60s, and '70s, IBM employed around 12,500 people who were housed in over six million square feet of plants, offices, and laboratories. Poughkeepsie was known as "Big Blue," and our life revolved around my father, Bill, being an employee. He and my mother, Anita, had moved to Poughkeepsie in 1953, the year I was born, to start a new life with my father taking a job as an IBM toolmaker. When asked as a youngster what my father did, I would simply say, "He makes tools, I'm just not sure what kind of tools." I thought hammers or screwdrivers. It was not until many years later, when he received the President's Award, did I realize that what he did was important in some significant way to IBM's success. Moving from their childhood homes in Mt. Vernon was a significant event and one that certainly changed the course of my life.

I was born in Mt. Vernon Hospital on July 30th, 1953. My parents were both devout Catholics, my mother being an Italian immigrant and my father Irish. Their parents were not pleased that they were moving seventy miles north of them, so weekend visits to Mt. Vernon became the custom. They would pile me and my two brothers and sister in our Chevrolet Impala sedan and make the trek down every weekend. We would first visit my mother's family who lived in a three-story tenement that housed my grandmother, my mother's brother, Primo, and his wife Connie and their daughter, her other brother, Louie, and his wife Fran and their three daughters and my grandmother's cousin's family. Three levels of pure Italian craziness. I loved going to visit them. We played stickball in the street, visited the small park up the road, but mostly we went from floor to floor tasting whatever each family was cooking for dinner. It was pure heaven. I loved their Italian food, and still do, and this was an Italian playground of food. Meatballs, sausage, pork chops, homemade ravioli and pasta, lasagna and more was always on the menu.

We would often sleep overnight, and I vividly remember sharing a bed with my cousin Carol and my grandmother, who spoke extraordinarily little English. We would squish into one full size bed and, somehow, it all worked. They lived in a three-bedroom flat with a common walkway through each other's bedrooms. Privacy was not a word uttered as their apartment was exceedingly small. We had some grand Sunday dinners after going to Catholic mass at St. Francis of Assisi Church, which was a short walk from their tenement. It was a very Italian-loaded parish and there was a sense of community, even though we lived seventy miles north. Us "kids" always had to sit at a separate table from the adults, or we ate first, as the dining room was tiny, especially with eleven kids between us all. Dinners would be loud with lots of laughter, yelling and people talking over one another. If my mother and her sister started talking in Italian with my grandmother, then we knew something important was being talked about and we hoped it was not about one of us. Food was plentiful, delicious, and truly Italian.

My Italian cousins were so much fun, and these were playful days, with the boys spending time mostly outside playing stickball, basketball or flipping baseball cards. The girls did their thing with dolls and the like, which I was always curious about. All of us got along great and enjoyed being with one another. Oh sure, we had our moments where we fought, called each other names, got yelled at, and occasionally got spanked, but that was what it was like back then. When my older cousins Patti and Elizabeth started dating, we loved meeting and being with their boyfriends.

My aunts and uncles were honest, hard-working and loving people. My mother's siblings, Primo, Louie, and Ida were living a dream having immigrated from Italy and living a life they would never have had if they had stayed in Italy, in the small town of San Nicandro in Abruzzo. They were thankful to be in America, and even though they were not wealthy, they lived their lives with appreciation for family and the small things.

My father's family were Irish and lived nearby in Mt. Vernon. My memories of my father's parents are not as vivid. They were older, and my grandfather liked to smoke cigarettes and drink beer while sitting in his rocker. I never liked to kiss him as he always had a beard stubble, and I did not like the way it felt. He was a big baseball fan, being a New York Giant fan before they moved to San Francisco. He became an avid Met fan and so did I. It was the one important thing we had in common.

My Irish grandmother was the cutest woman. She was so kind, friendly, and had a profound sense of humor. I recall once when she was eating dinner with us. She had this habit of chewing her food to get the flavor but would not swallow it, but rather would discreetly take a napkin and spit the remains of her bite of food into the napkin, which gradually became larger and larger. Well, I noticed it one evening and when my mother asked if I wanted seconds I answered with, "No, I'll just eat Grandma's napkin." Not sure what I thinking to embarrass her like that, but I had said it and could not take it back. Well, she laughed and realizing she had been caught handed me the napkin and said, "Here you go." Touché.

One of my uncle's was named Buzz and he was a Mt. Vernon firefighter. He was this bigger than life guy, who was boisterous and had remarkable fire stories. My brother John eventually joined the fire department and I soon followed. As he got older, he loved that we followed his path.

Life as a youngster growing up in Poughkeepsie with an awesome extended family helped me appreciate the value of family. I loved my life and never had any major crisis—except for this one habit that I had, which was wearing my mother's lingerie, which was not exactly something I could tell anyone about. Thanks to my father being an IBMer, we had the IBM Country Club in our backyard, and we frequented it often. During the summer, we would walk there for day camp to swim, play basketball or baseball, golf, and whatever else we wanted to do. It was a big playground, and we took advantage of it. The yearly dues were $3.50 per person per year. I never realized how good we had it growing up, but I certainly do now. Where else could a lower middle-class family find the kinds of activities this country club offered?

I played in the IBM little league baseball league, then in the Babe Ruth league before moving on to high school ball. CYO basketball in grade school with St. Mary's in Wappinger Falls helped me hone my basketball skills, as did the basketball court we had in our driveway. We were always playing pick-up games or HORSE and I became a decent basketball player. I had a great bunch of local neighborhood friends that hung out together. We would sit under a big maple tree in the Ornowski's yard next door and just stay busy with them or play kickball or catch on the street that separated our two homes. It was idyllic. It was a great neighborhood and our parents all got along. We were always outside playing Army in the summer or building huge snow forts in the winter. My life could not have been any better growing up, except for that one secret I had.

I started skiing while in high school when a fellow under classmate, Vicki Curatolo, who I had a crush on, asked me if I wanted to go skiing on a double date with some mutual friends. Little did I realize that because of that date my life would wind up revolving around the ski industry. I had never been skiing, but I was willing to try it. One snowy weekend day, we drove up to Belleayre Ski Center in the Catskill Mountains. The resort was owned by New York State and at the time was not exceptionally large or modern.

We got our rented skis and headed out to the lift. I managed to get on the lift without falling. But I was not so lucky getting off the chair and tumbled with her onto the ground. I then asked her, "Vicki, how do you turn? How do you stop?" She said, "Shape your skis into a pizza wedge and just go down the hill. You will figure it out. If you need to stop, you can fall into the hill and if that does not work, try to grab a tree." That was an immense help. Not exactly what a ski instructor might teach a newbie today, but with trial and error I figured it out and have been stopping the correct way now for over 50 years. It was magical, as it was snowing, and I was with someone that I wanted to go out with, and we were all having so much fun.

Shortly thereafter I took a day trip up to Hunter Mountain in the Catskills. I went with a good high school friend, Steve Franklin, who unfortunately would die at the age of twenty-four in a tragic accident. He was a crazy, fun-loving guy and a good friend. He had no fear, nor did I, so it seemed only logical we would go to the top of the mountain on our first run. There we were, dressed in our Wrangler jeans, complete novices trying to go down a steep black diamond slope. It took us forever and we learned a big lesson. The rest of the day we stuck to an easy green trail called Broadway.

Hunter Mountain was a New Yorkers mountain. It was built by two Jewish businesspeople, who I would get to know very well over 20 years later. Lots of people from NYC and surrounding counties would come up for the day. It had a great bar where many a Rheingold beer was consumed, as they were the major resort sponsor. It was famous for its yearly New York City Fire Department ski race where a team of five firefighters, dressed in full turnout gear, would ski down with a 100-foot length of two and a half-inch hose through a gated course. It was so funny to watch as many participants would wind up being slung out from the whiplash of being at the end of the hose. After many years of not allowing fire departments outside of the city to participate, they created a second ski race for those departments in upper New York. It was a big drunk fest and a yearly event for me for many years.

I met my first wife, Lorraine, in high school and after being just "good friends" we started dating in late 1971 while we both were starting college. Her family were skiers, which was exceedingly rare back in those days. Over Christmas of 1971, I was invited to join her and her family at a ski chalet at Killington, Vermont. I jumped at the offer and got to spend time with my girlfriend and ski the largest ski mountain in New England. It was a snowy week, and we skied every day. I recall skiing Snowshed Mountain, which was,

and still is, some of the best beginner's terrain in the ski industry. Little did I realize that Killington would eventually become my go-to mountain for many years before I would eventually wind up starting my ski career there.

Skiing has been a big part of my life for over 50 years. One of my prized possessions is a chain necklace with all my season passes, starting with my first pass at Killington in 1983 through the present day. It is so funny to look at these pictures and see the aging process and, obviously, the biggest change of all when I transitioned in 2016 to being Cami.

I love golf, but not as much as skiing. I always have said, "You can always leave a ski mountain feeling good about your day, but you can't always say the same about leaving the golf course." Both are unique in that both sports are always just you against the conditions. Both are great sports, and I am truly thankful to do both and as often as I do, which over the past 25 years has averaged over 60 days per year for each sport.

In 1971, when I was eighteen, I began to realize how dedicated my brother John was as a volunteer with the nearby Croft Corners Fire Company (CCFC) where he had joined two years earlier when he was 20 years old. He would back his red Camaro into the driveway so that when he needed to respond at night to a call, he could just pull out without having to back up and lose time in responding. I admired his dedication, and I wondered what the job was all about. A plectron, which was a radio that would alert you to a fire call, would often go off and away he went. It was intriguing to me, so I asked him questions and eventually he hooked me in. I was 20 years old and still in college.

I immediately jumped in with both feet and attended the Dutchess County firefighter's class. I loved the thrill of driving and/or riding in Engine 5, our main attack rig. I would also say that fighting a fire and being the person in the lead into the room on fire is a feeling like no other. I had become addicted. I was working at the Merit Department Store at the Hudson Plaza and would often dart out to a fire during work hours. People really liked the volunteer firefighters in the town and supported us in many ways, and we were admired, not frowned upon.

Living at home, I did not do the typical college fraternity thing, as the firehouse became my fraternity. We had an excellent group of guys who were deeply committed to the work, and I was continually active for many years. John and I would often hear the call, jump into our turnout pants, and race to the firehouse, which we could get to in three minutes (driving amazingly fast, of course). We would jump into whatever rig was left and away we would go. It was thrilling.

I became highly active as I had time to commit. A tradition in the company was to track attendance on a big white pin board. If you made a fire, call you got a red pin. If you made an ambulance call, you got a green pin. It was easy to spot how active each of us was. If you hit three hundred total calls for a year, it was a major accomplishment. It carried some prestige to be among the leaders. In those days we had some big fires. It was not unusual to fight a house fire or a large brush fire monthly. The adrenaline that flowed when responding or working the fire was addicting. Sometimes you would be the driver/pump operator, or a hose man, or a ladder man, or a truckee, but whatever it was, I embraced it. Your role was often determined by what rig you jumped on when you got to the firehouse. Back in those days we would

ride on the back step of the engine, holding onto a polished metal railing. It was a thrill hanging on for dear life as the rig sped through town. Those were the days. It was a rush!

Driving our old ladder truck, known as Truck 2, was a challenge. It was a 1955 Oren convertible with a 50-foot-long banger wooden ladder, which required a few firefighters to raise. It was a huge beast to drive and required lots of strength to turn its steering wheel. The brakes on it went out more than once and required some skillful driving, and I was fortunate it never happened while I was driving.

I was one of the ring leaders of a group of young aggressive firefighters. We became known as the "Young Turks" by the older guys. We prided ourselves in doing excellent work, but we also knew how to have fun. What was life changing was meeting some great guys to whom I became remarkably close. It only takes one serious fire to build friendship and loyalty. I quickly learned who I could depend on. Our friendships continued to build as these same people became part of our social relationships as well. Wives and girlfriends became part of the firefighting family. Lots of social events like dances, fundraisers, parties, and softball kept us all together quite often. We would travel together to a parade/convention and stay in the same motel, having memorable times, and these parties became legendary. My kids grew up with their friends being other firefighter's kids.

As part of the "Young Turks" I was aggressive, proud, and energetic. My confidence in fighting fires was never higher. I was a good firefighter and did not have many fears in taking on any fire. My biggest fears were being caught at home dressing up in my mother's clothes.

1976 was the 25th anniversary of the founding of Croft Corners Fire Company, so two years earlier we had decided to host the Annual Dutchess County Parade and Convention. Me and my best friend at the time, Dave Walsh, took on the challenge of painting every hydrant along the convention parade route red, white and blue in whatever way we wanted. What turned out to be a cool idea wound up to be a ton of work, but we got the project done and I proudly paraded by each hydrant with a sense of purpose.

The highlight of being a volunteer was access to the ready room, which was another name for where we sat and waited for alarms to come in. We always had the most current and largest TV at the time to watch sporting events. The best part was that we had an old soda machine that we converted into a Pabst Blue Ribbon dispenser for twenty-five cents a can. We would often go there after work or after a call and have a few beers together It was like having our own bar. I was still in college at the time, and this was like having a fraternity of friends to drink with whenever I wanted. I did not miss living on campus at all as I had my own circle of good friends. The firehouse became all-encompassing, and my love of firefighting grew.

It was a natural for me to want to become a paid firefighter and it turned out that I would be the first volunteer from Croft Corners to become a "paid man." I had taken the civil service exam and fortunately came out #2 on the exam out of all that took the test. The fire commissioners offered me the first position that became available, and I accepted, starting June 1st, 1976. I was so proud of myself.

I was assigned to an excellent group led by Lt. Art Rose. In the group were Rich (Fish) Fishwick, Bill (Billy T) Tompkins, and Ed (Dolly) Madison. We worked out of the old Arlington Fire District headquarters on Main Street in Poughkeepsie. It was an old firehouse, complete with a brass firepole we would slide down to access the rigs from our upstairs bunkroom. I recall one night when we were called to respond to a house fire and I hit the pole, which I had done many times, but let go too early and hit the ground hard. I knew something was wrong, but I jumped in Truck 1, which was a diesel Seagrave 100-foot aerial. It had so much power and was a thrill to drive, especially through town with lights and siren blaring. I started driving and was in severe pain and said to my lieutenant that I thought I had broken my ankle. He looked at me in amazement and asked, "How?" I told him, "I let go of the pole too early." He told me to pull over and he took over driving, but it was an embarrassing moment, made worse by, as it turned out, a sprained ankle.

Each night, one of us would be assigned to sleep in the dispatch room. We would answer calls that came in overnight and then dispatch the equipment needed. We would set off a tone that would activate plectrons of the firefighters in the district. I vividly remember the call wording being, "Attention Arlington receivers- First alarm, 18 Marwood Dr. Engines 1, 5, and 7 and Truck 2 respond." Eventually a new headquarters was built, but the times in the old one will never be forgotten. We would have water fights with hoses, drop water from the second floor on the unknowing down below, and other shenanigans, like testing new volunteers. We would tell them to strap on a ladder belt, and then we would hang them from the front rung of the ladder truck and tell them to try to unhook themselves and get off the ladder. Well, unless you were Superman, it was almost impossible to do. You would have to pull yourself up with one arm and then unhook the belt. While they struggled, we doused them with water. It was a sick kind of fun.

I will never forget the words of Lt. Art Rose, one of my first true mentors when I first was hired. He could see my talent and he knew I had gone to college, which no other paid firefighter had accomplished. "T J," he said (my nickname), "you will have to pay your dues around here for a while, but you will get places. Work hard and smart." Great words to live by and to which I did and still try to do.

There was a lot of friction between the volunteers and the paid men, but I was able to bridge the gap and remained a highly active volunteer with Croft Corners as well. I unabashedly can say that I was an above average firefighter and was completely involved in all aspects of the job. I took numerous fire service and EMT courses. I went to many classes at the New York State Fire Academy in Montrose, N.Y. I was slowly building up my knowledge base and when the position of AFD Municipal Training Instructor

came up, I applied and was promoted.

I took this position knowing full well that most of the firefighters on the job hated training. They thought they knew it all, so my job was challenging, but I was persistent and held the line. The district never had a computer, so I bought an IBM word processor and would do my training outlines on it, so they could be reused. The volunteers and I got along great because I was still considered one of them. My personality was extremely outgoing, and I enjoyed giving training presentations and public speaking. It would serve me well later. I received an extra stipend for doing this job and would still serve on my shift as well. My future was bright, but I wondered if I would ever use my degree in Business, on which I was sitting.

My brother John had become and is one of the most prolific firefighter and officers in Arlington Fire District history. He went through the ranks, starting at lieutenant, then captain, then Asst. Chief of Croft Corners, then Chief of the District, then Fire Commissioner of the District, then chief again, and after 48 years retired in 2018 as First Assistant Chief of the District. He was the most dedicated firefighter that Arlington has ever seen, and I am immensely proud of him. He remarked to me after he retired, "It was a great 48 years, saw lots of action, fires, horrific accidents, and was proud to serve the community."

In the early 1980s, he and I were tight and the real power players in the district. He was Assistant Chief at Croft Corners, the busiest volunteer company, and I was Municipal Training Officer for the district and oversaw training of all paid and volunteer firefighters. I was recognized as an aggressive firefighter. I was President of the Firefighters Union Local 2393. It was good that I left when I did as he and I were on a collision course for who would hold the top position at some point down the road. I was destined to eventually become deputy chief for the paid staff side, just as he was heading to be chief for the volunteer side, which meant I would report to him. Luckily, I left the fire service and John went on to an amazing career without any competition from me.

We had some very funny times over the years. Like others in the company, I eventually got into the CB radio craze when it was hot. Each of us had a handle, with mine being Hockey Puck Car 1, which was referring to my old 1959 Red Volkswagen Convertible that I would drive to fire calls. I can remember we got drunk one night and about ten of us started driving it around, with some guys hanging off the convertible top and one friend on the hood of the car. I even drove it into the back room of the firehouse and did wheelies. The stuff we did in cars was crazy. We never gave a lot of thought about driving drunk as it just was not something we were afraid of as we knew the local police officers.

We began hosting carnival/casino nights with gambling and rides, and families loved it. We made a lot of money but worked hard to make it. For years I was chair of this annual event and worked hard to grow it. After a night of this work, we would start drinking beer. Some of us heard about a new thing called the Bat Race, which is when two teams square off with each player drinking a glass of beer and then running down to where someone is holding a bat on the ground. The player then had to circle the bat three times with his forehead on the top of the bat and then run back to touch another player's hand where all this was repeated. Now this may not sound terribly hard, but we played it on a hill and sideways, which resulted in us falling downhill when running because we were dizzy. It was hysterical.

Firemen's parades were always a special day for us. Arlington Fire District was recognized as one of the county's best marching departments. The highlight every year was the Hudson Valley Firemen's Convention parade, which was held in various towns each year, but the parades held in Saratoga, Lake George, and Lake Placid were always the most fun. It was a long weekend of pure debauchery. There was always a Friday night Mardi Gras parade where we would dress up in costumes. One year we were the Smurfs, with all of us dressing in blue and white, including white tights, which was of course welcomed by me. We won first place and partied like crazy. I was always in the color guard, proudly carrying the American flag. It was an honor, but I must say that at times we stepped off with quite a buzz after drinking beer for hours before. We would anxiously await the judges results at the end and we typically placed in the top three, but when we took first place, it was quite the accomplishment. Our uniforms consisted of red wool shirts and blue pants, worn on the hottest of summer days and were a true test of our will power. Our families would be part of these weekends and resulted in our friendships growing even closer. We fought fires, answered emergency rescue calls, played softball, raised fundraising money, drank beer together, and became one close group. Our slogan was "Aggressive and Proud."

I became good friends with Dave Walsh, who was my age, who went to Marist College as well and he and I were like brothers. We were inseparable and we often went out together at night to local bars. We did everything together and he wound up working at the IBM Country Club athletic office with me. We were good firefighters who were totally committed to being productive volunteers, and for years we were among the most active leaders on the tracking board. He was nicknamed OJ, because he always drank orange juice. Somehow, I got nicknamed TJ, which had no significance other then we spent time together. In 1975, we both took the exam for paid firefighters in Arlington. I wound up scoring number two, while Dave was three out of all those that took the test. I was hired first, and Dave quickly followed. We double dated with our girlfriends and hung together all the time. He was my first male best friend. Unfortunately, when I left for the ski industry our friendship was hard to maintain and we have barely spoken over the years. Dave continued at Arlington Fire District and became Assistant Chief for the paid staff and a community college fire service professor. There are people I miss in life and Dave is one of them. I've yet to call him personally about my transition, although he is aware as I sent him a note when I first transitioned. There are few people I would be humbled while telling and he is one of them.

Dave and I spent a lot of nights at our favorite bar, the Holiday Bowl-a-Mat in Wappinger Falls. What a great bar it was. We would most often dance and listen to a great cover band called Lenny Frank and the Rhythm

Rockers, who played songs of the Doobie Brothers and the Eagles. It was a pickup bar, and over the years I did some picking up.

I can remember meeting one extremely attractive woman who lived in nearby Coldspring. She was Italian, which was a plus. Although I was seeing Lorraine, she was away at college. I found her interesting and asked her out. For our first date, we decided to play tennis because she said she was, "really good" at it. I picked her up at her home and even met her parents, which I was not expecting, and then we went to the town tennis court in Coldspring. She was wearing a cute, white, frilly tennis outfit and looked amazing. We took opposite sides of the court and I hit her the ball. Her racket never moved. She stood there and started laughing. She said, "I don't have a clue how to play tennis. I just wanted to go out with you." She completely bluffed me. I loved her humor.

We continued to date occasionally, which I knew was risky. I took her to the Monticello racetrack one night to bet on the harness races. My car had been worked on earlier in the day at Rube's Gas station, owned by my good friend Jack Cohen, a member of the firehouse. I picked her up, and on the way over we were driving on I-84. Unbeknownst to me, the hatch on the hood of the car was not completely closed from the work earlier in the day. A gust of wind hit the car and the hood completely ripped off and it flew over the roof, bashing it in along the way and then landing on the busy highway. It all happened so fast that there was nothing I could do about it. I circled back to try to find the hood, which I did. It was completely dented in and damaged. I managed to get it off the highway, ducking sixty-five mile per hour cars, and left it on the side of the road. She and I continued to the track and still had a fun night. We were so lucky that it did not smash into the windshield and hurt us. I was dating her on the side, so I am lucky to have gotten away with it. I ended the relationship shortly thereafter when I realized that Lorraine was a far better choice for me overall.

I could write a lot of stories about my experience at Croft Corners. In summary, it was an amazing time in my life as I grew into an adult. I was attending Marist College and the firehouse became my fraternity house, since I lived at home. It was an honor to have served this fire company as I did, including being treasurer of the company, for many years. I helped negotiate the purchase of the Krakower property with my brother, which turned out to be a real money maker for the company, as we leased the land to the IBM Corporation for a large monthly amount so they could use it as a parking lot for their buildings nearby.

My brother John was the most active firefighter in our company and he and I were always involved in raising money. One year, he and I were approached by a guy who had been trying to sell his house, unsuccessfully, for an extended period, as interest rates were over 15%. He came to us with an unusual offer to create a raffle program: sell 2,000 tickets at $100 each. He wanted $150,000 from the proceeds, meaning we would net about $50,000 before expenses, which included a large party where the winner would be picked. It took us many months of work, advertising, and sales, but eventually we sold them all. It was the first house raffle in New York State, and unfortunately it would be one of the last as the state decided it was no longer acceptable to auction off houses in this manner. We had accomplished something bold and progressive, and it was a highlight of my years with CCFC that I would never forget.

When I turned thirty, my wife and I made the decision to move to Vermont. I left my job at the Arlington Fire District and resigned from being a volunteer at Croft Corners. It was quite the 11-year run and stands out as one of the best periods of my life. Many great friendships were made, great times were had, and fires fought.

I have no regrets in spending 11 years of my life and career serving the Arlington Fire District. If I could do it over, I would. I have a great deal of respect for firefighters and proudly can say I have three retired NYC Battalion Chiefs as good friends here in Park City. They have said they never thought they would be friends with a transwoman, but they are.

Like most paid firefighters, we always had side jobs during our days off and I was no exception.

Bill Dean Jr. was an older, but active volunteer firefighter with Croft Corners, and we became friends despite a large age difference. He owned a union trucking company and hired part timers, like firefighters, to supplement his crews who worked at IBM facilities moving offices and equipment. Once I was hired, I got paid the union wage of $13.75 per hour despite not being in the union. He would pay us in cash and when he gave out the envelope you would think he was doing you a favor, which in my case he was. I remember when I was buying my first house and I needed to earn extra money for the down payment. I had asked Bill as a favor to get me as much work as he could as I needed a certain amount for the deposit to pull off the purchase. When I had reached the amount I needed, which I had told him about, he looked at me and said, "Ok, by my count, you got what you needed." Indeed, I had, and he had me in the palm of his hand knowing that he had helped me out. He was a tough businessperson, but at the end of the day, a good guy. He respected me, and I respected him. He wrote an amazing letter of recommendation for me when I applied to Killington that I still have to this day. I cannot help but wonder what his reaction would have been if he found out I was transgender.

I would often help another firefighter, Barry Ireland, who had his own roofing company on the side. It was tough work, and, in the heat of the summer, just brutal. Putting a roof on top of an old roof was not too bad, but if the old roof needed to be stripped off, it was backbreaking work as you would use a flat shovel and jam it under the old shingle and pry it off. I quickly learned that there had to be an easier was to make money on the side.

Since I had a degree in business, I thought that I could do taxes on the side, so I took a tax preparation course. I started my own tax business and would do people's taxes and charge them accordingly and it worked out well, as I could do it from home.

I liked the idea of using my accounting degree, so I ran for and was voted in as treasurer for Croft Corners Fire Company in 1975. I was fairly compensated for my monthly bookkeeping services, as it was at a time when the fire company was prospering. This was a great part-time job, but only one of many extracurricular jobs I had while I was a firefighter.

When the opportunity to buy a successful vending company with cigarette and candy machines came up, Dave Walsh, a good friend and fellow firefighter, and I became partners. Our primary account was Vassar College, where we had both cigarette and candy machines in each dorm. It was a cash business, and the money was good. It was the perfect side job as we would take turns restocking the machines and be able to work around our schedules at work.

One day I was down in Newburgh picking up candy and cigarettes from my wholesaler. He was Italian, and Dave and I always suspected he was associated with the mob in some way. He led me out back to where I could pick up some candy. We walked through a room where his people were stamping cigarette packs—illegally, I might add. I was surprised he had walked us through, and he then said, "You didn't see any of this, got it?" In a small way I thought because of that I was a part of his mafia clan and that if I ratted him out, I would be killed. I never said a word and I am still alive.

How does someone who is a paid firefighter also become a TV producer of a sports channel called Hudson Valley Sports Productions?

Back in 1981, I was good friends with a fellow volunteer firefighter at Croft Corners Fire Company by the name of Bob Grosch. Bob was the first real entrepreneur that I had ever met, and he had the gift of salesmanship like no other. He was a graduate of the New York Military Academy and was also still active in the Army Reserves. He was a mixture of someone who was fun, eccentric, serious, smart, ambitious and I could go on and on. We became fast friends. He was about five years older than me, but that did not matter. I fought many a fire with him and he was a beast to be with as he was a little hyperactive, which can sometimes be extremely dangerous, but he was always willing to work hard and do what he could do as a volunteer.

A family Christian broadcasting company on aerial antenna Channel 54 was started during the early 1980s. They had purchased a huge TV production trailer that was used at the 1980 Olympics from ABC. They needed to raise funds to help pay for it and offered it for rent to qualified TV production companies. Bob decided to partner with someone with some capital, Rich Lewis, a local Hudson Valley entrepreneur. The business plan was to rent the truck to produce various sporting events of significance in and around the Hudson Valley, hence the name Hudson Valley Sports Productions.

Bob brought me on as his producer as he recognized my talents and he felt I could use them for more than just being a firefighter. If I'm being perfectly honest, I did not have a clue about how TV production worked, but I would soon learn fast enough. I took on the role of helping to find sporting events that we could televise and produced a list of events that we thought might be worthy, including Marist College Basketball, West Point football, and the regional Little League World Series competition.

During the baseball strike of 1981, we broadcasted the first fastpitch softball game to be televised (to our knowledge) anywhere between the long-time local team known as the Poughkeepsie Brewers and the Franklin Cardinals, formerly the Raybestos Cardinals of Stratford, Connecticut. The Cardinals won the low scoring game, but our production got great reviews.

It had become a long, sizzling summer, and we realized quickly that we might have come upon something that was of interest to all TV baseball watchers who had been deprived of baseball since June 12th. Over 1,900 fans watched the game in person, the largest crowd ever to watch a fastpitch game. This was the first long strike in baseball history, and people simply missed baseball and a fast pitch softball game would suffice. T

We knew we had a gem in the rough after we showed the broadcast and we produced the idea to Warner Wolf, who was the New York City Sports announcer for CBS TV. I reached out to him on the phone, and I told him what we had to offer.

He was interested enough to say, "Come on down, bring a tape, I'll look at it and if it's good, I'll consider using it." Bob was ecstatic. He and I got in the car and drove down to the CBS network headquarters in Manhattan. We were escorted into Warner Wolf's videotape room, where he watched numerous sports tapes to pick out something of interest for that night's broadcast. He was my favorite sports announcer and I watched him daily. When he said, "Let's go to the videotape," sports fans paid attention, as he always showed great sports plays. We handed him the tape and he stuck it in one of his video machines and up came the game on his television. He watched it with keen interest. He looked at us and said excitedly, "This is fucking awesome. I'm playing this tonight."

So here we were, complete novices in the TV sports production world and one of our first broadcasts was going to be featured on Warner Wolf's Sports that night. We were overwhelmed with joy. He quickly edited the tape to the minutes he needed and said to us, "Meet me down in the broadcast area and you can watch the broadcast live." We were thrilled and sat with eager anticipation of what was to happen.

Little did we know that what we had provided would turn out to be something more. Warner opened his sports spot with the proverbial, "Let's go to the videotape, from up in Poughkeepsie, New York where the Poughkeepsie Brewers are playing the Franklin Cardinals in fast pitch softball."

Clips of the pitchers were shown. Warner added, "The stars of the team are the pitchers and for the Poughkeepsie Brewers, its long-term veteran, Cliff Ong. The pitcher for the Cardinals is long-time fastpitch veteran, Owen "The Fog" Walford, who has been recognized as one of the fastest and best fastpitch softball players in the world."

More video clips were shown of The Fog striking out batter after batter. These guys could sling a softball with almost blinding speed. The strikeout ratio by both pitchers was high. They were simply hard to hit. When a batter was lucky enough to hit the ball, it was a bullet towards either the defenders or an open space for a hit. The game was extremely fast paced. The fields were small with 60 ft. base paths.

Baseball fans needed baseball and Warner Wolf was enthralled. At that point, Jim Jensen, who was the lead newscaster, jumped into the conversation with Warner and said, "This is great stuff." He then asked Warner, "Is it possible if my team of CBS News All Stars could play the Cardinals and face "The Fog" in an exhibition game for the benefit of the charity we support?"

Bob and I looked at each other in amazement. Warner Wolf looked at us while on the air and yelled over to us, "Could you guys try to arrange that?" From off camera, Bob answered "Of course," without giving it a lot of forethought. Jensen and Warner went on and on about it for a while and how cool it would be. It was one of the highlights of the newscast that night.

We left on cloud nine and could not wait to see it on video tape. I had asked my wife, Lorraine, to tape the show and when I got home, I watched it with great excitement. I even took a couple pictures of the TV screen of Warner and The Fog with our Hudson Valley Sports Production logo proudly on the screen, that I still have.

I was also instrumental in negotiating a deal with West Point Academy to broadcast various Army collegiate sports, including Army football games in the fall of 1981. I was quoted in the Poughkeepsie Journal on September 17, 1981, as saying, "The Academy is pleased with the prospect of the Army intercollegiate sports program being aired on local television. To our knowledge, this is the first time the local viewing audience will be able to see regional, first-class collegiate sports on a continuous basis. We are trying to make Army sports a household word like New York Giants football and Yankee baseball."

We eventually broadcasted Army football and Marist basketball that winter. Unfortunately, the station, WFTI-TV, was underfunded and was forced to close in early 1982. Without the mobile TV production truck, we were out of business as well. It was quite the run while it lasted.

As I look back on this, it seems ironic how this little local startup TV sports production company, with management that had no prior sports production experience, could pull off what we did in such a brief period. We were truly on the cusp of starting something big. I realized all big dreams can end just as quickly as they start. It was unfortunate as TV sports shows were starting to go big time, thanks in part to the startup of ESPN in September 1979.

Some firefighters have some crazy part-time jobs to supplement their firefighter job, but this one took the prize. It was too bad it had to end, but I learned a lot of valuable business experience, thanks to Bob Grosch. It was the beginning of me having the confidence to leave the fire service only two years later and really start my business career.

My "Career" Using Pot

I had managed to avoid smoking pot throughout high school and college. I always had a sense that it was not for me, because at the time it was illegal. The first time I had exposure to pot was when my mother was cleaning my brother Jim's room, or should I say, snooping around in his room. In the back of his closet, she found a bag of marijuana. I was in my room laying in my bed as I was not feeling well and had stayed home from class at Marist College. She came into my room and asked, "Tommy, what is this?" and pointed to the bag of pot she had found. I asked to smell it. I knew immediately that it was pot, but like all good brothers should do, I tried to protect him and said, "I think it's the tobacco that Uncle Primo (my mother's brother) smokes in his pipe." She was smarter than I gave her credit for, and she said, "No it's not, it's marijuana." So, poor Jim had been caught and suffered the consequences. I had my first experience with pot, but still was not interested in smoking it.

In the middle of the summer of 1975, I was going to my first union meeting for the Arlington professional firefighters local 2393. I shared a ride with two fellow firefighters who were around my age and worked on the same shift. They were great guys named Rich (Fish) Fishwick and Pat (Patsy) Rose. Both would go on to have very distinguished careers in firefighting. I got in the backseat of the car and those two were in the front. Pat casually lit a joint, which surprised me. He passed it over to Rich, who took a hit from it. Rich tried to hand it back to me, but I was not taking it. He turned to me and said, "Here, take a hit." I replied, "No thanks, I don't smoke pot." Rich looked at me sternly and said, "Well, now you do."

After my first hit it was obvious then I enjoyed the feeling marijuana gave me and some 46 years later, I am still smoking marijuana, although I now prefer edibles. I have smoked pot the entire time. I have smoked with my friends, family, and total unknowns, and do not look back on it with any regret. I view marijuana as being the same as liquor. Liquor can get you high or drunk. Marijuana gives you a feeling of a high or euphoria, which can be better than alcohol. Given a chance to further legalize it, I am voting in favor of marijuana, although that is not likely to happen in Utah, as our Mormon legislature would never allow recreational use.

Over the years, I have had a lot of crazy experiences while smoking pot with others. Although I do not condone some of my actions, they happened, and it is time they be told.

One of my craziest pot stories occurred back when I was a firefighter with Croft Corners Fire Company. I had been a volunteer for a while and then became a paid firefighter in the same fire district. I used to love to play in the firefighter's softball league. Croft Corners had a good team, and I was the shortstop. We loved to play against Rochdale Fire Company, which was another Company in the same district, so there was a lot of rivalry. I knew many of those guys and worked with some of them.

We played on Friday nights during the summer, and it was nothing more than a big party with a softball game involved. Our wives came with our growing number of kids. We enjoyed food and drink, but the games were serious to us.

Following one game, myself and another volunteer, Bob Grosch, drove back together to the firehouse. On the way there, I pulled out a joint and we shared it. It was not the first time I was stoned and hanging around the firehouse. However, it would become unusual for me to take the next step. We were drinking draft beers when a first alarm came in over the plectron for a house fire on Sheraton Drive. This house was near my parent's home and identical to the house my parents owned and that I once lived in.

My brother John, who was Assistant Chief at the time, took off in his chief's car, also known as Arlington Car 10. There were not many firefighters that were qualified to drive the 100-foot-long ladder truck identified as Truck 2. I looked around and realized I was the only one who was approved to drive it. Without much hesitation and while stoned and after a couple of beers, I jumped behind the wheel and took off to the fire scene. It was a crazy thing to do. I could have been fired from the district from a job that I absolutely loved.

What follows is even more crazy. I got to the fire scene with no issues. I had been driving my car stoned for years and it really did not affect my driving, but one could easily claim my senses were impaired. John, my brother, arrived on the scene and reported a working fire with flames coming from the master bedroom on the first floor. He's then said over the radio knowing that I was driving, "Truck 2, it's the Feeney's house. The fire is in the master bedroom. Grab a one ½ inch line and head in." He knew he could have full confidence in me to go put the fire out.

I jumped out of the ladder truck after parking it and donned a Scott pack, which was a breathing device that firefighters use to go into smoke-filled rooms. I prided myself in being able to do it in around 30 seconds and went on easily. I went up to the front door and saw that my brother had pulled an inch and a half hose-line off the engine. He went as far into the house as he could without a Scott-Pak before dropping most of it in a pile in the living room. I entered the house knowing exactly where to go to fight the fire.

The fire was hot, intense, and smoky. I went in on my hands and knees following the hose line that was coming out of the house in hopes of finding the nozzle. But I wound up crisscrossing over the hose line and I inadvertently headed back out the front door.

John saw me and yelled, "What are you doing?" to which I sarcastically replied, "Obviously, I can't find the nozzle." I quickly made another attempt, and this time found the nozzle and moved towards the bedroom where the fire was intensifying and still blowing out the windows. I opened the door and quickly doused the fire with a good amount of water.

A problem was developing as I was wearing only sneakers, not my fire boots. The power to the house was still live, so I wound up getting shocked from the electrical current, as I was standing in water. I was yelling loudly for someone to cut the power, which eventually happened, but not soon enough for me. We cleaned up the scene and returned to the station, but not a word was ever said on my part as my brother would have been so mad at me. My brother John never knew any of this, unless he reads this book. Somehow, I had managed to survive a very eventful fire and one I would never forget.

In 1985, I was playing in a golf tournament called the Ice Breaker at Lake St. Catherine Country Club in Poultney, Vermont, which was right near my home on Lake St. Catherine in Wells, Vermont. I had become good friends with a local golfer named Larry Wayne, who lived in Fair Haven, Vermont. We often teamed up in member-guests and other tournaments. We were playing in this invitational against a couple of golfers who came over from the Rutland Country Club, Ricky and Joe Bove. They were great guys, Italian, and fun to play with. They were also good, and we knew we would have a tough time in the nine-hole match with them. It was a beautiful spring day with foliage starting to peak. Larry and I often smoked pot while playing, but we discussed it before and decided that we would hold off until the outcome, either way, was known.

We went into the eighth hole down by two, and Larry anxiously asked me, "Do you want to smoke some pot? It can't hurt us at this point." So, he pulled out the joint that was stuck around his ear and lit it. He and I proceeded to start to smoke it. We asked Ricky and Joe if they cared to join in and, surprisingly, both took hits off the joint. We did not really know if they had ever smoked before. It turns out that it affected them far more than it was affecting us. They became very loud, outspoken, and funny and lost focus for sure.

Meanwhile, our game got better as they went in the toilet. We easily won the next two holes to force extra holes. They were still feeling the effects when we won the first extra hole, and the match was over. We had won! At the after party, they did not let us forget that they lost because of us offering them some pot. Ironically, 20 years later, I saw them both at a tournament in Rutland Country Club and both brought up the story. We shared a good laugh over what had happened. Of course, they completely blamed Larry and I, and rightfully so.

"I'm On Fire"

Around 1978, we were dispatched to respond to a fire call at a dormitory at the Oakwood Friends School near the Croft Corners fire station. Oakwood School was a private college prep high school founded by the Quakers. It had been around for many years and was built high on a hill overlooking the IBM main plant in Poughkeepsie. Most of their dorms were large structures made of brick and wood and had been used for many years.

The fire was really going (another way to say for "seriously on fire") on the second floor of the dorm. I was with one of my fellow crewmates, Billy Tompkins, or as we called him, Billy T. He was a great guy and always had a profound sense of humor and would certainly never do anything intentionally to hurt anyone.

The fire had moved into the attic, and we were pulling ceilings on the second floor to try and get at it. We were in a dorm room and Billy was pulling part of the ceiling down. When it fell, it fell on me, and it came with sheet rock and debris that was on fire. Unfortunately, I had not done a good enough job of closing my bunker coat up to the top. Quickly, I found myself with embers down the back of my neck. I immediately started to scream and run out of the room into the hallway and down the hallway, which was filled with water from all the firefighting efforts.

My brother John, who was captain at the time, turned an inch and a half hose on me. It knocked me down onto the hallway floor where the water was six inches deep. I managed to crawl out to the front door where I exited screaming, "Help, I'm on fire!" A lot of fellow firefighters saw me and could see that I was panicking. They quickly realized that something was really the matter. The embers were hard to find inside my shirt and stayed hot and kept burning my skin. It was extremely painful, and I was really scared.

I was loaded into the ambulance and raced to the emergency room where I was treated for second-degree burns. Fortunately, there was never any lasting scars, just the remembrance of the fear I had for that moment. I wound up with some days off at home to recuperate, which was never a terrible thing.

I realized the most important lesson, which is that I thought I was invincible as a firefighter. I learned quickly I was not. I would run into burning buildings when others were trying to get out. I was in my twenties, had two young daughters, and I never gave a lot of thought to the fact that I could end up with a severe injury or even die on the job. I was always trying to be the "hero." I think that fire and getting burned had an enormous impact on me from that day forward, as I looked at things differently as to what risk I would take. I was more cautious than in my first years on the job. When the next signal came my way, it would change my life forever.

I caught a job (another term for a working fire) one night while off duty in a neighborhood home. The house was the same Cape Cod home as my parents owned. My brother John, who was then Assistant Chief of CCFC, was quickly on scene and told me where the fire was. A volunteer and I made an internal attack with an inch and a half hose-line. We quickly dosed the fire and by all accounts it was a clean, fast knockdown and I could be proud of our work.

The next day, a picture of me was in the local newspaper, The Poughkeepsie Journal, taken by a local photographer and friend, Judy Weiner. It was of me taking oxygen from a tank after the fire. I was sweaty, dirty, and obviously one might assume I had been working hard to extinguish the fire. Behind me in the picture was a typical road sign, very clearly visible, hanging over my head. It was a DEAD-END sign.

It struck me immediately that there was a hidden message in that picture that I needed to heed. I loved being a firefighter, but I had been sitting on my business degree from Marist College and always felt I should pursue other options. For the first time, I felt like I was in a DEAD END career, although I was doing well and had become the Municipal Training Officer for Arlington. My future was bright in the fire service. I was confused as to why I had the feeling that I needed to change careers. I was also finding myself wearing my wife's clothes more often. It comforted me despite being 180 degrees different from who I appeared to be, which was a rough and tough firefighter. I remember wearing a G-string and nylon hi-top socks on a night shift and hiding it from my crew in the bunkroom.

Right after that time, I got a call from my good friend Rob Dunne. He told me that Killington Ski Resort was hiring for an internal auditor position. I was so naive that I had to look up what an internal auditor even did for a business. I sent in my resume and a handwritten letter to apply for the position. That move would change my life forever.

Pop Warner

In the early 1980s, I was asked by the captain of Croft Corners, Gil Brewster, if I wanted to be an assistant coach on a Pop Warner football team of which he was head coach. Gil was a great guy, an incredible firefighter then fire captain, well-liked by everyone, and a big no-filter Camel cigarette smoker. The team was called the Eagles, and we played in the Town of Poughkeepsie Pop Warner league. The kids ages were from 9-12years old. Gil had picked and developed an incredibly talented group, and we knew we had a promising season when it started. I had never played football in high school, but rather was the head grandstand cheer leader with a fellow classmate, Donna Jo Tortorella. I followed pro football and was a New York Giants fan. I knew the game well, so I was not hesitant to say that I would help.

Our team had a great quarterback in John Sala Jr., who could throw the ball with speed and accuracy and would later go on to quarterback the high school team. We had powerful running backs, strong linebackers, and a strong work ethic, driven by Gil's leadership. He was like the Vince Lombardi of Pop Warner football. I must admit the excitement of coaching these kids was exhilarating. We had weeknight practices and games on Sundays. For two hours each Sunday, I had the opportunity to coach and impact the lives of these young kids, and it was an extremely rewarding experience. Three years in a row, we were a powerhouse and won the league championship. It was another bonding activity amongst us firefighters, as the coaching staff included two other members of the firehouse. On a much smaller scale, we felt like we were in the National Football League.

"My Water Broke"

On October 7, 1978, I was at the Spackenkill High School varsity football game on a beautiful, sunny, fall Saturday afternoon. I had driven the ambulance from Croft Corners to the game to be on standby for injuries. Another volunteer, John Lentz, was with me. I loved going to the football games as many players I had coached in Pop Warner played on the team. On this day, I asked Lorraine, my 9-month pregnant wife to come with me, as she often did.

The game was in the third quarter when suddenly Lorraine came running out of the stands and over to me at the ambulance. She had a concerned look on her face as she came up to me. She said, "Tom, my water just broke." I asked, "Where?" She said, "While sitting on the grandstands. We've got to go to the hospital, now!" Today, I have always wondered who ever cleaned it up?

We ran over to my red Jeep Cherokee that she had driven to the game. I was concerned about her wet pants damaging the upholstery and asked her to not sit on the seat directly. I do not even want to tell you her response, but you can just imagine.

We headed off to the hospital and I must admit I was driving like a madman. Once there, they quickly got her through the emergency room process and into the delivery room. She began the long, arduous task of delivering our first daughter, Erin. It was taking a long time, so I took a break from my Lamaze responsibility to go check on the Yankee playoff game. I recall the excitement I had when the Yankees won and went rushing into her room to share the news. "The Yankees won!" Here she was, crying in pain and the last thing she cared about was the New York Yankees. Her response was direct and to the point, "I don't give a SHIT about the New York Yankees!!"

Erin was born shortly thereafter and has become a life-long Yankee fan. Obviously, it was embedded in her from day one. As tradition in the fire company, all my friends and I went out drinking to celebrate. At 25-years-old, I had my first daughter, and I was thrilled.

Lorraine and I loved skiing and were renting winter homes around Rutland and Killington for a few years when we bought some land at Lake St. Catherine near Poultney, Vermont and started building a second home. It was then that I heard about the position at Killington Ski Resort and applied. Surprisingly, I got hired and I resigned from the fire service to be an internal auditor for a whopping $13,000 per year. I had been making over $30,000 per year as a firefighter. I rationalized the move by thinking that, with our newly constructed house, we would not have a mortgage. After I got hired, I looked up in one of my college accounting books what I should expect to be doing as an internal auditor. It sounded interesting and looked to be a great training ground for future growth and management possibilities.

I started in July 1983 and had an office on the ground floor of the main Killington office building, alongside the cash room. My supervisor was a great guy named Allan Wilson. Later in our ski careers, he and I would share similar ski industry paths. My first main assignment was to write standard operating procedures (SOPs) for departmental functions involving financial and operational controls. I learned a lot about how various departments ran and developed relationships with many supervisors. Since my job included audits and involved pointing out where something went wrong in a department or how it could be improved, I was not always the most liked person, but I did my job and did it well. I wrote a lot of procedures in a short timeframe and was acknowledged for it.

In late January of 1984, I was summoned to the office of the controller, Marty Wilson, who had hired me. He was a larger-than-life boss, and I was nervous when I would meet with him. Later in my career I would realize he had become my mentor and someone I learned a lot from being around. I walked into his office and with him was the assistant. controller, Bob Fenner, who was one of the nicest people I would ever have the privilege of meeting, and Bill Ghent, the accounting manager. On the desk was a pile of computer paper stacked two feet high. The lodging department had installed a new IBM reservation, check-in, and back-office software a month earlier, and we had no clue how to book the daily results. Marty looked at me and said, "You need to figure out what is going on with this mess. Stay on it until it is all cleared up."

It was my new assignment and would turn out to be over three months of tedious work. Upon finishing, I walked into Marty's office and gave him the results. I said, "Well Marty, the bottom line is that we will have to write off $243,000 of unearned revenue that was mistakenly booked." I thought he was going to explode through the roof. When he finally calmed down and I told him how it happened he looked at Bob Fenner and said,

"What should we do?" Bob said, "I suggest that we promote Tom to a new position as Lodging Accounting Manager and let him keep a handle on all this." Marty agreed and my career in the ski industry took off.

It was exciting to build a new department and I hired some experienced staff in various roles to make things run smoothly. I relocated my office to the Lodging Center and spent the next three years in the position. Eventually, I was invited to attend the weekly senior management meetings and present a weekly update on the financials of the lodging department. It gave me exposure to the president, Hank Lunde, the CEO, Pres Smith, and other vice presidents. I became recognized as a capable financial analyst, and it would lead to more opportunities down the road.

We settled in Wells, Vermont where I commuted over fifty miles for my new job at Killington. I was quickly solicited to join as a volunteer when the word got out that I was a former paid firefighter. The department was well-run with good leadership, albeit it was Vermont style. I lived close to the fire station, so I often drove a rig to the calls. My prior experience proved to be of value, and with my business background I was asked to run for president of the company. It was a pleasant experience, and I am glad to have been able to help. In 1987, we had a new home built and I moved the family to Clarendon, Vermont and I said goodbye to an excellent group of guys.

Once I was established in the fire company, I heard that the Vermont State Fire Division was looking for training instructors, so I applied and was quickly hired. The training courses I had previously taken were extensive and were invaluable to help get me hired. and I enjoyed instructing other Vermont fire departments. Unfortunately, when my workload at Killington increased, I left the training position to open it up for someone with more time to do the job.

I did other things to supplement my income, including doing the books for a friend of mine, Rob Dunne, who had started a large construction company that built condominiums at Stratton Mountain in Vermont.

I loved basketball and played in the Rutland Recreation League for years. I played on the Back Home Café team and developed many close friendships over the years. When a class came up to learn how to be a basketball official, I took the course, which was quite fun. I never refereed a varsity high school game, but I did do some JV games. I was extremely critical of my officiating after a game and would feel bad if I felt I made a bad call or missed a call.

Real Life Rescues

In summer 1985, Lorraine, me, and our two daughters, Erin and Lindsay, traveled to just outside Denver, Colorado to visit my wife's brother's family. We visited for a few days and had a blast.

Being in the ski business, I was curious about Aspen Ski Resort, so we took a couple of days to check it out. It was beautiful, and I could now understand why it was so popular. On the drive back to Denver on I-70 to catch our plane, a car passed us at an extremely high rate of speed. My wife and I looked at one another in amazement and I muttered, "Crazy bastard." Sure enough, within a couple of miles we came up on that same car rolled over on its roof. I quickly pulled over and we both got out of the car to see what we could do to help. Our firefighting and nursing occupations would come in handy. We could see him trapped inside the car, as well as a young child. There was no fire or smoke, but the situation was critical. Back in those days there was no smartphone, so we had to depend on other Good Samaritans to somehow get the message to the fire rescue and police.

In assessing the situation, which was becoming critical, as they were screaming for help, the only option was to try and pick the car up enough that we could get the passengers out. Other drivers came upon the scene asking me what they could do to help. I quickly huddled them up and said, "We have to pick the car up!" We made the decision that the three other men would try to pick up the car and that I would go underneath and try to pull the people out.

Their adrenaline kicked into gear and, sure enough, the three guys picked up the car high enough so that I was able to crawl underneath and get the people out a window by herding them out one by one to Lorraine. I never gave a thought to the fact I was putting myself at risk and that my life was dependent upon three guys holding up a 3,000 lb. car, but they did it. I would love to bottle adrenaline and sell it.

The police arrived and took my information and statement. He thanked me for my help. I asked the trooper if I could leave the scene soon as we had a plane to catch. He said, "What time is the plane?" I told him, "An hour and a half." He said, "You'll just make it, so step on it." He even gave me his name to use in case we got stopped for speeding. It was odd that we had just gotten permission to speed after rescuing some people who were in an accident caused while speeding. Lorraine did not let me speed, but luckily, we still made the plane on time, but barely.

I felt good about what I was able to do to help in that situation. I had put my own life at risk to help others. I felt a true sense of accomplishment. Lorraine was immensely helpful as well in caring for the injured when they were pulled out. Her nursing skills came in handy. We had done a good deed and felt good about it as we flew home.

Over my sixteen total years of active rescue and fire service both paid and as a volunteer, I did everything someone in the rescue/fire service could do. I had saved people's lives from fires, I had rescued people from cars, planes, and ditches, I had given mouth to mouth and kept people alive, I had delivered babies and I fought some amazing and dangerous fires.

I will never forget the day when a guy came walking into Arlington Headquarters while I was working, carrying a box of Dunkin Donuts. We were all watching TV with our feet up on hassocks. I looked at him and asked, "Can we help you sir?" He said, "No, you already did. Don't you remember me?" I looked closely and replied, "No sir, I don't." He said, "Two weeks ago at Heritage Garden Apartments I had had a heart attack and was dead on arrival and you revived me with mouth-to-mouth resuscitation. I just wanted to say thank you to you." I looked at him and jokingly said, "Well, you lived, that's great!" Unfortunately, those of us in the fire service were not particularly good at following up on whether a patient lived or not, so it was nice to hear that he had.

My greatest firefighter accomplishment was that I taught others how to be a firefighter as a municipal and Vermont State Fire Training Instructor. I had always felt good in knowing that I was teaching and helping others. My ski profession business life would prove to be equally as exciting as my first career.

In March 1986, I was leaving work at Killington on my daily commute home to Wells, Vermont from the resort, which took me about 50 minutes. I was driving down Route 4 towards Rutland and was in Mendon when I was startled by what I saw happen in the opposite driving lanes. I looked to my left and saw a car crashing into the back of a slow moving 18-wheel tractor-trailer. The car plowed right under it at a high rate of speed. I could not believe what I had just seen. I immediately pulled over and ran over to see if I could help. My body was flowing with adrenaline. I could look in and see the body of a man, who had been decapitated upon impact. I looked in the car for others in the car and could see no one. I could only stand back and wait for help knowing that there was nothing I could do to help him. Ten excruciating minutes later, the fire department arrived, and I withdrew from under the truck, so they could do what they needed to do to extricate him. It was a horrifying situation and very gruesome and the worst accident scene I had ever seen, and I had seen many. I was visibly shaken when a Vermont state trooper came up to me and asked if I was okay. I was in shock when I said, "Yeah, I'm fine." He thanked me for my help. He took all my information and asked me to describe what I had seen. It was a scene of horror that to this day I remember vividly.

I drove home in complete shock of what I had just experienced. Lorraine greeted me as usual, and I had to tell her what I had just seen and done. I cried, and she hugged me. She was proud of me and knew I was suffering. I could not get over that I felt a certain sense of helplessness as there was not a thing, I could do for him. It turns out that I could do something and would in upcoming days.

A Great Friend Lost

I met Rob Dunne in 1976 while my first wife Lorraine was working with Rob's wife, Londa, an LPN where they both worked in Beacon. They discussed a trip together to the South Lake Tahoe area to go skiing. Rob was not my friend at first, but we became fast friends on the ski trip. He was fun, gregarious, a great storyteller, and a great skier. We skied Heavenly after a six-foot snowstorm that came after a winter-long snow drought. It was an amazing day of skiing and the beginning of a great friendship.

Rob and Londa loved Vermont and wanted to move there. They bought a building lot in Mt. Holly, which was about 45 minutes from Killington Ski Resort. They wanted to build their dream home, which would be a log home, and they started construction in the early 1980s. On weekends, Lorraine and I would drive up to help them build and to ski with them. When Linday was born in 1978, we asked Rob to be her godfather. He loved to have her sit on his lap, and he would bounce her on his knee. He loved Lindsay and she loved him only as a child could. I remember one night when new were sitting in his long cabin style family room with a roaring fire going playing Backgammon and Lorraine started nursing Lindsay while sitting on the couch. Rob bet her that she could not squirt her breast milk across the room. Now, I had never seen her do anything even remotely this bizarre, but she willingly said, "You're on." At first, she struggled, as getting distance was difficult, but once she figured out the proper angle and technique, she easily was shooting her milk across the room and won the bet. I kept a picture of her doing it for the longest time, but for some reason it disappeared.

Lorraine always had an enthusiastic sense of humor and, once, it got us both in big trouble while in high school when we were good friends, although we did not date. Our Catholic class went on a field trip to the local Jewish temple in Poughkeepsie. Lorraine LOVED to laugh, and when she did, it could be loud and for a long time. I was sitting behind her in a pew when she started to laugh uncontrollably. It was contagious and I started to laugh. It was very noticeable, and it was a clear interruption while the rabbi spoke. Father Farley, our teacher, and the priest who married us four years later, was not happy. He called us into his office and read us the riot act. He demanded we write a letter of apology, which we did. I am lucky he did not hold it against me as a few months later he wound up recommending me for a McCann Foundation Scholarship, which I received to cover a four-year full scholarship to Marist College, including books.

A lot of other firehouse friends would come up to their house in Vermont as well, and they all became good friends of Rob and Londa. A weekend in Vermont would always bring great memories of skiing, drinking, building, and eating big meals around the wooden table with bench seating, which was such a pain in the ass.

One day we were installing his wooden floor using a floor hammer. If you have never done this, give it a shot. It is not as easy as it sounds. We were cursing so badly that the women all got mad at us, telling us to knock it off. So, being young entrepreneurs, we started a swearing penalty fund at $.25 per swear. We quickly filled up the jar and used it for drinking money that night.

Rob started his own construction company in Mt. Holly. When it was our turn, he helped us build our home in Wells, pro bono. His favorite line was, "Close enough for government work," and he used it whenever a saw cut came out a little off the mark. I became his company accountant making sure employees and vendors got paid. He was growing fast and landed a big condominium job at Stratton. He had moved into the construction big leagues and the pressure on him was great to keep it all afloat.

In the 1980s, cocaine was the rage. We all smoked pot, but this one guy introduced our group to coke, which to me was something I had sworn off. I did it a few times and liked the high I got, but not the cost of it. At some point early on I stopped, but Rob did not. He tried to escape the pressure by drinking and doing coke. He got hooked and used cocaine often.

On a cold winter's day in March 1986, he got high one night after work and fell asleep early. He had started a fire in the huge stone fireplace but did not put the ember guard over the opening. Londa was home, but at some point, she went out to the store and left the house. More than likely the opening of the front door when she left caused a gust of wind to come down the flue, blowing an ember out onto the floor. The living room caught on fire. Rob was soundly asleep on the second floor. He did not stand a chance with it being a log home. They found his body lying in a red antique claw foot tub in the bathroom. Lorraine and I had given them the tub as a housewarming gift. Speculation was that he was trying to get out of the house through a window over the tub. I remember Londa calling me to tell me. I do not think I have ever felt as sick to my stomach as that night. I had lost one of my best friends in life at only 33 years old. We were all devasted. Rob was the life of any party, dinner, or ski run.

Londa asked if I would give the eulogy at the funeral home during the wake, and I said I would. The next day, I closed the door to my office and began to write and cry and cry and cry. As I wrote, I realized my words were touching and heartfelt, but could I speak to them in a public setting? I had never experienced death like this. The death of someone you genuinely love like a family member. It was exceedingly difficult and an emotional time for me, as a couple of days earlier I had gone through the decapitation episode. I had experienced two tragic deaths and my emotions were spent.

That night, I was home working on the eulogy when the phone rang. I answered the phone and a gentleman on the other end explained to me that he was the father of the young man who was killed in the car crash. I was immediately taken back and wondered why he would call me. I would quickly find out when he said, "I hear you were a witness to my son's accident. I got your contact information from the state troopers." He then asked me, "What did you see? Was he in pain?" I thought to myself, how am I going to answer him? I was in mourning and grieving the death of my best friend in life and I am now being asked to tell a stranger my story about his son's tragic death. I told the man what had been going on with me and that it was difficult for me to tell him what he already knew.

I mustered enough courage and gingerly said, "Sir, I'm sure you know that your son's head was decapitated." He stuttered and said, "Yes, I know, I am just wondering if you thought he suffered?" I offered, "It all happened so fast, he didn't have time to suffer. By the time I got to the car under the trailer he had passed."

I knew he had died catastrophically, and it was hard to produce more soothing words. I was now in tears and so was he. We chatted about his son, and he told me what kind of man he had turned out to be. He thanked me for taking his call and said, "I feel relieved. Somehow talking to you will help me move on." We hung up and I cried for his loss and mine. It turns out that I had been helpful to him, which I could not be for his son.

Unfortunately, I still had to deliver Rob's eulogy. I worked diligently on what I could say that was appropriate. He had a lot of friends, and we were all in shock over this tragedy. I had to represent them all and my words needed to be meaningful. I locked myself for a second day in my office in the lodging office building where I worked. My staff were sympathetic to my loss and continued to leave me alone. I wallowed in my tears and scribbled out my thoughts. It turned out to be a beautiful and memorable tribute loaded with touching and funny stories. My voice quivered as I spoke my words of compassion. I broke into tears at times but managed to pull it back together enough to finish. It was one of the hardest things I had ever done at that point in my life. I had lost my best friend to a fire, which had been my career for years. The irony was not lost on me. I was young when my grandparents passed away, and I did not fully understand death at that time. At 33 years old, I quickly came to understand death and its consequences.

I was truly emotionally hurting. For the first time in my life, I experienced death to such a degree that it would take me awhile to recover from the emotional scars. Lorraine was always there to help me. I have always felt that a good cry is therapeutic, so I had a lot of therapy that month. My daughter Lindsay lost her godfather at 8 years old, and Lorraine and I lost our best friend. Vermont was never to be the same. Life would be different without Rob in our lives.

In 1986, I was still working at Killington as the Lodging Department accounting manager, and we had installed a new IBM software reservation and check-in system. IBM was hosting a conference for users of the software in Atlanta, Georgia in early April. I asked for permission to attend so that we could stay abreast of the latest technology and improvements and to make recommendations on how to improve our operation of the system. My request was approved, and I flew down to Atlanta knowing full well that the Masters Golf Tournament was being played only 150 miles away in Augusta, Georgia. I looked at the schedule of events and figured out that on Wednesday, April 9, before the tournament started, I could rent a car, drive down to Augusta, and hopefully scalp a ticket to get in to watch the practice round. I did just that and drove down to Augusta and was able to secure a ticket and badge for the grounds. I was absolutely thrilled to be able get in as I was a big golfer and loved to watch the Masters. I walked the grounds in utter amazement of the beauty. I decided to follow Greg Norman and Jack Nicklaus, who were playing together in the practice round. It was quite a thrill to be able to see Jack and Greg, who was close to being the number one player in the world at the time. I watched shot after shot in full amazement of their abilities. They did have a bet of some sort going on and it appeared that at the end of the match Norman had won. The course and grounds were gorgeous. Flowers were blooming at their peak and the birds could be heard chirping in the tall pines. It was like walking on sacred ground.

Augusta National is full of nostalgia. I found it interesting that even back then they would offer egg salad sandwiches on white bread with the crust cut off for only $1.50, and to this day, they still do. In fact, their food menu has rarely changed. It was special to have been there and even more special for the fact that Jack Nicklaus won the Masters at 46-years-old that year, with an amazing fourth round that ranks among the top finishes ever in the Masters. I was home by then and watched it on television, but it was just like I was there that day that he won. It was one of the golf highlights of my life.

In 1986, I was asked to join the Board of the Junior Achievement Center of Rutland. This was a great organization with an important mission statement, which was to educate high school students about economics. I was very engaged and loved supporting their work. I went to Rutland High School and taught the students economics using the curriculum Junior Achievement provided. The students loved that I worked at Killington as controller, and it gave me credibility. I discovered that I really enjoyed being in front of kids and teaching them. It was a wonderful experience and gave me confidence to do more public speaking as time went on.

Around this same time, I was asked by a fellow Junior Achievement Center Board member, who was also a volunteer with the American Cancer Society, to help organize a golf fundraiser called The Longest Day of Golf. I asked a good friend, Mike Rotella, owner of Rotella Building in Rutland, John Coscia, a Killington Base lodge bartender, and Andrew Farbman, the food and beverage manager at Snowshed Base Lodge, who were some great guys whom I had worked with at Killington to join me and we formed a foursome.

The object was to start playing at daybreak and play until nightfall and get as many holes in as possible. This had not been done before in Vermont, so we did not know what to expect. Friends and family were solicited to make pledges per hole played. We started at around 5 a.m. at the Killington Golf course on June 21st, the longest day of the year. We each had our own electric carts to get to our ball as quickly as we could, so we could hit our shot and drive to our next shot. On some holes we would race up to the tee box, quickly line up, and on the count of three, hit our shots at the same time. We could play through other foursomes, who, when hearing what we were doing, cheered us on. At first, we were ecstatic and pumped, but as the day went on, we became irritable with one another. We ran out of things to talk about and got on each other's nerves as the day dragged on. We stopped talking and just played more golf. It was very tiring, hot, and playing that much golf lost its fun and appeal. But we kept playing and playing and playing, while eating and drinking on the run.

As dusk approached, we were joined by friends and family who kept cheering us on. It was getting dark, but we had set a goal that we desperately wanted to achieve. We were running to hit the ball and racing around as fast as we could. We marched triumphantly up the 18th hole at around 9:30 pm after 16.5 hours. We were exhausted, but we felt a sense of accomplishment. We had just completed 108 holes, or six full rounds of golf, and raised over $3,500 for the American Cancer society. A beer never tasted as good as it did that night after we adjourned to the outdoor bar at the lodging center. Our friendships were solidified. I do not remember what I shot per round as it was not important, but I felt a true sense of having done something special that made a difference.

Pico

I had been friends with Ken McEwan, the head tennis pro at the Killington Tennis School while working in the lodging department. He must have recognized my talents, and in 1987, he offered me a position as the controller for a condominium development company he was partners in at a neighboring ski resort, Pico Ski Mountain. He offered more money and although I did not really want to leave Killington, I jumped shipped and took the job. The company was building condominiums at the base of the resort with retail on the lower levels. It was not terribly challenging, and I was able to take on other roles while there.

While at Pico, I saw an opportunity to start a new business in a developing ski tourism field, which was to take pictures and videos of people skiing on the mountain and then sell them to the clients. I called the business Pico Visions. The concept came from an established business at Killington that did very well, so I jumped in and bought a used film processing machine. The thing was monstrous in comparison to today's technology, taking up a space that was 15x20 feet. I hired this eccentric manager and a couple staff members and was excited for its growth potential.

Since I had purchased the needed machine to develop the pictures at Pico, I called on the owner of Jiminy Peak Ski Resort in Massachusetts, Brian Fairbanks. I had skied there often while a firefighter in New York and loved the mountain. He heard my pitch and was intrigued and agreed to lease me some space in the lodge for a percentage of revenue. I set up shop in the base lodge and named the business Jiminy Visions. Although we had some busy days, it barely paid the bills. During the second season, video was introduced thanks to the JVC recorders I bought, but that did not help enough, so I closed both shops after two years. However, I was loving being an entrepreneur, so it was time to bring on another business adventure.

I had developed a close relationship with a good friend in Rutland, Mike Rotella. He was married to a woman named Barbara, who was very athletic. She wanted to open a workout facility in town, and they asked if my wife Lorraine and I wanted to be partners. I do not remember how I produced the money, but I did, and we became partners, along with another major general contractor in Rutland named John Russell. He had the influence and the money to make it work. We built the place out and it came out quite nicely. This was way before gym facilities became the rage and it was fun to be a part of this business.

While I was at Pico, the development group was building a health facility to service the condominiums we were building. A good friend and golf partner, Larry Wayne, was the project manager and worked for Rutland

Group out of Rutland, Vermont. The project was progressing well, and the walls and roof framing was starting to come together. One weekend in mid-summer a violent rain and windstorm roared through the resort and the walls and roofing came crashing down. It was a complete disaster and took months to get started again.

In the fall of 1987, I got a call from Marty Wilson, the SKI LTD. Chief Financial Officer. He said, "Tom, we just bought Bear Mountain Ski Resort in California and have asked Alan Wilson to go out there and serve as controller." Alan Wilson had hired me at Killington years earlier, so I said, "That's great. He'll do an excellent job." Marty said, "That's not the only reason I called. We want you to come back and serve as Manager of Operational Controls at Killington." I was floored. This position was effectively the highest fiscal management position for Killington and reported to Marty. I had not been gone from Killington for even a year, and wase offering me a huge pay raise. I did not have to think long about it as I had already realized that the position at Pico was a dead-end job and not challenging enough. I quickly accepted. I missed Killington and loved working there, so it was great to go back to a place I loved. I would be very responsible for the financial success of the resort, so it was a fantastic opportunity and that would lead me to even better positions.

I was officially promoted to controller at Killington after a year, but effectively the position was the same as before. I had two offices; one was in the upper administrative offices and was between the offices of Pres Smith, the CEO of SKI LTD., and Hank Lunde, the president of Killington and had a splendid view of the mountain. The office was in the lower administrative building which housed my staff and others in the accounting and IT departments, and Marty Wilson had his office there. I did not particularly like working in that office and spent most of my time at the upper administrative building, though I checked in on my staff often. One woman, Ann Richards, was an excellent worker and worked her ass off. I worked a lot with the IT department in trying to improve various reports that we used. We closed our Profit and Loss statement weekly, including all revenues and expenses. We budgeted for the year on a weekly basis and after the week was closed and the reports run, I would analyze them and make a presentation at the Thursday morning management meeting. I was my own boss for the most part and would come and go as I wanted. I took advantage of skiing often and would walk up the hill to the Killington chair and to get some runs in. I was also the chief enforcer of not selling lift tickets to others. I had been doing it myself for years when we would go up for a weekend. I would buy a two-day ticket, get drunk on Saturday night, and then try to sell the Sunday ticket in the parking lot. I knew how to catch culprits and loved to scare them and tell them they could be arrested for theft of services. Of course, I never actually called the police, but it was a good bluff. It was a dream job in the ski industry, and I was a rising star in the company.

During the summer months of 1988, Hank Lunde, who was president of Killington, divided the management team into groups with specific topics to examine for potential additions and changes to Killington, like a daytime grooming center and food and beverage improvements. I was put in charge of one that was to determine if we should allow snowboarding at Killington. My group looked at all aspects of allowing it, including its potential profits and impact on skiing operations, with an emphasis on how snowboarders will negatively affect trail conditions such as changing mogul configuration. Our neighboring ski resort, Pico, was the only one in Vermont allowing it, but before anyone could go on the mountain, they had to check in and demonstrate their proficiency. Snowboarders just loved that hassle. It was crazy what the initial reaction to snowboarding was in the ski industry. They were truly treated like second-class citizens.

Pres Smith, CEO of Ski Ltd., had no interest in allowing it and had already said such, so going into the evaluation we knew we had an uphill battle. Following months of meetings, we decided to recommend allowing snowboarders. We made our presentation, which included a proforma that indicated we could make an extra $1 million in profit in year one. The management team all concurred. Hank Lunde then said to me "Sell it to Pres or it's a dead idea." Yikes! He was tough to approach, especially on issues he felt strongly about.

I needed to find the right time to approach him and that occurred by happenstance. I was in the cafeteria food line in the base lodge at Rams Head and Pres was just ahead of me ordering. I said, "Hello" and out of the clear blue and without forethought, I blurted out, "Pres, how would you like to make an extra $1 million in profit this coming year?" He responded, "Well of course I would." I then responded, "Then you should approve snowboarding." I immediately felt that I tricked him, and it could backfire. To my amazement he did consent to having me make the presentation to him, which I later did. It was hard to dispute the fiscal impact and he realized the time had come to allow it, so reluctantly, he agreed. He specifically instructed me to remain in charge of the new program and be responsible for how snowboarders adhered to skiing etiquette.

When the season started, snowboarding became a huge hit. Snowboarders had their first major eastern ski resort where they could board. Despite the obvious success, Pres persisted in his dislike, and I got more than one phone call while he was out skiing that those snowboarders were blocking a trail (and their favorite was the lower headwall of Superstar where they congregated and which I could see clearly from my office windows). He would bark, "Get up here and clear them out." I guess for some reason he thought that was punishing me. I loved to go out skiing and did not need a reason, so I gladly went as directed. He also directed me to stand in front of the ticket windows at Killington Base Lodge to count and track how many snowboarders were buying tickets to validate our projections. By the end of the year, there would be no turning back on our decision as we easily exceeded our projections.

In some small way, because of my work on this project, I feel that inadvertently I had a lot to do with the expansion of snowboarding. Of course, Killington would have eventually succumbed to the pressure to allow snowboarding, but my work helped accelerate it. I was not alone in this process, but I certainly took on the most risk and responsibility. To this day, I feel proud of my involvement as snowboarding has become 30% of the total ski and snowboarding market.

While at Sugarbush Ski Resort later in my career, I continued to see the value in snowboarding and asked my senior management team to learn how to snowboard if they did not already know how. We all participated in a training with our snowboarding instructors. It was a great bonding experience, and we had a good laugh at our failures and successes. I was not particularly good at it, despite having skied for almost 30 years. One beautiful sunny day while off duty, I ventured out to the slopes to practice on my own. I felt I was starting to get the knack of it until I started down to the base area, which required me to board on a flat trail. As I neared the bottom with a ski lift overhead, I took a bad fall when I flipped over as quick as you can imagine. I was immediately in pain and yelled out an obscenity that begins with an F and ends with a K. A woman and her child were riding the lift and saw me fall and heard me yell out. Luckily, I was not wearing my resort coat, but rather my own ski jacket. She yelled down, "Are you okay?" I sheepishly yelled back, "I think so." I went down to my office and told my staff what had happened. The Ski School Director asked me what caused the fall and I told him I was not sure. I was simply boarding down the slope. He asked, "Were you riding on the edge of the board?" to which I replied, "No, should I have been?" He replied, "Yes, it's like spreading butter on a piece of bread. If you don't keep the knife on a slant the bread will rip." I replied, "I guessed I missed that part of the instructions." The result was a shooting pain down my arm from a pinched nerve for a year and a half that hurt like hell almost every day. I had learned my lesson and I have never been on a snowboard since and that was 1998.

Although my history with snowboarding was initially positive, I have come to dislike snowboarders while I am skiing. The noise they make, the speed they go at, the way the terrain is affected, and their rudeness at times makes me wish I never had gotten It started at Killington.

In 1990, as part of the Killington senior management team, my coworkers and I were all assigned additional operational responsibilities. I was placed in charge of overseeing the Killington Base Lodge (KBL), one of many Killington base lodges and the largest, serving as the hub of the resort. I coordinated food and beverage, ticket sales, the rental shop, ticket checking, the retail shop, customer service, and job-sharing staffing between all these departments. If something went wrong during the day, I needed to deal with it. If I had to have a part time job, this was one of the good ones. It was a blast to run a busy lodge loaded with fellow New Yorkers and Massholes, as many skiers commonly called skiers from Massachusetts. I was very well known in the lodge by the regulars. There was one woman who always ignored me. She was an avid skier and would show up early each morning. I wanted to meet her, but she was standoffish. She would eventually become my wife.

I particularly enjoyed helping at the lodge by being the bar-back at the Mahogany Ridge Bar at KBL on Saturday afternoons. It was a little hole-in-the-wall bar underneath the main staircase. It was always packed, and it was mostly a crazy, drunken scene by 4 p.m. I recall more than once the bartenders and I having whip cream fights with customers after selling too many shots of Jägermeister. The song of the ski season was Love Shack by the B-52's and it would set the place on fire when it came on. One of my favorite and best bartenders was Pat Murphy, a long-time bar employee who on certain weeks would make more than the president of the resort did thanks to the huge tips he would get. He was a Killington icon.

It was a good people watching bar with people looking for that perfect ski partner. I can remember seeing a very striking but unknown woman at the bar one late afternoon. Our eyes met, and we caught each other looking at the other. I was immediately attracted to her.

I vividly remember one very snowy, dark Sunday afternoon I was talking to skiers seated in the base lodge over the loudspeaker system. "Hey there Killington skiers. So, the good news is that the snow is expected to continue at a heavy pace overnight. We are expecting a total accumulation of two feet or more by tomorrow morning. If you feel so inclined to use, we have prepared an excuse letter for you to give to your boss explaining your Monday absence, which states that Killington had two feet of snow overnight and you do not feel comfortable driving in that much snow. Also, if you show today's ticket for a ticket for tomorrow you will get 50% off that lift ticket." The skiers roared with excitement. I am sure I was the first one in the skiing industry to use the loudspeaker for marketing efforts. We did wind up giving out a lot of letters and I remember that day being one of my top ten ski days.

I have a habit on social media of always saying a great ski day is one of my top ten ski days ever, mainly because I cannot remember each days' oddities that make it one that stands out. So, what is a Top 10 Ski Day? One thing for sure is that I have had some spectacular days with sun, warm temperatures, deep powder, or perfectly groomed runs. But it is not always the conditions that make a ski day great. Certainly, the comradery of friends and family on a ski day can also make it a top 10 day. I have had some incredible days skiing Killington when the conditions were not ideal, thanks to friends and family.

One day in 2013 I was invited as a guest on an early morning First Tracks outing. I woke up to over a foot of snow at my house, so I knew the canyons would show much higher snow totals. The resort reported twenty-four inches overnight. We got there at 7:30 a.m. and were immediately ushered up to the Red Pine Gondola that American Ski Company had installed when we bought the resort in 1997. A total of eight of us with guides would ski the mountain for a good 75 minutes before everyone else. It was pure ecstasy. The powder was light and skied easily.

Another top 10 ski day was at Powder Mountain in 2012. A friend had won an auction for a day of snowcat skiing, which is where you ride in a large cab to the top of the mountain, and I was invited. It is a half hour ride on a good day, so we had to start incredibly early as we were looking at a major snowstorm. Most smart skiers would have bailed as the driving was treacherous, but not us when we had a cat day on the horizon. We all got there safely to a ski resort that has the lodge and starting point from the top of the mountain. It was still snowing heavy when we loaded up. This ski experience is vastly different from the norm, and we all had major butterflies. Up to the top we went. It is hard when visibility is bad and you are skiing an unknown mountain, but thanks to guides in the front and rear we found our way to some spectacular runs with deep powder. Deep powder skiing is hard. You work muscles you normally do not, and your wind is tested like never, but the euphoria you feel while floating down a trail is incomparable. It is a high unlike any other.

Back in 1997, Les Otten, the Chief Executive Officer of American Ski Company, and I took our bankers out to Squaw Valley in Lake Tahoe on a bit of an exploratory trip as we felt the mountain might be available to purchase. Les was a good skier, but not all the bankers were up to his level. Off we went from the top to the legendary KT-22 trail, which is recognized as one of the most difficult ski runs in the country. We easily got to the start of the run and peered over the edge. I felt fear like never before and quickly realized not only was this run not for me, but not for some of these bankers. Les was determined to show off and down he went with only one other follower. I quizzed the remaining group as to who wanted to ski it or walk back up with me to something less steep. Six of them joined me and we never looked back, except in knowing that we were still alive.

One busy, cold mid-winter Saturday morning, I was standing in front of the ticket booth at Killington Base Lodge thinking I might be able to answer questions, give directions, and generally help the customers. I would often spend time at the ticket booth to help a ticket seller, if needed. As controller, I was also the individual that set policies and ensured they were being adhered to, including one that stipulated that ticket sellers should check for signatures on the buyer's credit cards and if absent, ask for proof that it was the buyer's, which was easily accomplished by simply showing a driver's license.

I was close enough to one window to hear a transaction getting a little heated. What happened was that the seller noticed that for this one transaction the buyer had not signed the credit card, so she asked him to show proof it was him. He responded, "Well that would mean me going back to my car for ID, which is too far and what I don't want to do. You'll have to believe me that this card is mine."

Upon his refusal she called me up to the window to help resolve the situation. I asked for the credit card and then looked at him and upon seeing the name on the card I told the seller to complete the transaction, which she did. When he left, she looked at me in amazement and said, "Tom, you write these policies, and you just went against your own policy." I then explained, "Well, I looked at the name on the card and then I looked at the person. I noticed something that made it obvious to me that he was the legitimate owner."

"How's that?" she asked. I replied, "Well, his name was Edward Kennedy Jr. and I happen to know that he is more commonly known as 'Teddy Jr.' He is the son of Senator Ted Kennedy, and had his leg amputated after coming down with bone cancer at 16. Well, when I looked at him closely, it was obvious he only had one leg, so I was quite sure it was him. Kind of like, "If the shoe fits wear it." Proof that there are times it makes sense to go against rules. We both had a good laugh over it.

I was working during the winter of 1990-91 at Killington when my first wife, Lorraine, and I started having difficulties in our marriage. I cannot pinpoint any one specific reason for the problems and eventual breakup, but money and debt issues were high on the list.

Another was that we had been together since 1971, either as a couple or married (16 years), and the magic was gone. Our sex life became a second thought. We had given birth to two beautiful girls, who were then 12 and 10 years old. We struggled with the decision, but we separated in late 1990.

Luckily, I had the option to move into a condominium at Killington that I co-owned with my brother Jim, so I did. It was difficult, and I will never forget telling the girls our decision. It was heartbreaking and at the time my future seemed very bleak. I had an excellent job but feared what a divorce would bring.

At that time, management personnel like myself were asked to take on a second role and I oversaw the Killington Base Lodge operations, so I spent a lot of mornings there making sure things were going as expected. I can recall that the first time I saw this woman, who would turn out to be my future wife, was at Mahogany Ridge and I do remember thinking "WOW, she is beautiful." Our eyes met quickly, but that as all.

I was separated and had realized that I needed to have a woman in my life. I noticed her pattern, which was to show up early to ski, but always by herself. I was fascinated by her. Her hair was dark with some silver streaking, and she was strikingly beautiful (and still is). She loved skiing and skied most of the day. I wanted to meet her and since I was legally separated from my first wife, I set out to do so. I felt uncomfortable approaching her in the base lodge, but the opportunity finally arose one winter day.

I was out free skiing at the Bear Mountain area of Killington. I was wearing my red Killington jacket, indicating that I was a manager. I saw her in the lift maze, a good thirty people in front of me. I set out to catch up with her and started to pass skiers ahead by saying that I was management and needed to get by. I just barely got on the lift with her and sat next to her, skiing onto the chair before it left the load area. I was nervous but struck up a conversation and asked her where she was headed. She said the Needles Eye Mountain area to which of course I said, "I'm going to Needles Eye as well." I took a few runs with her, and we hit it off. Teri was a strong skier and still is. We swapped some stories about ourselves. When I left, I told her I would see her around. I was smitten for sure. She was a registered nurse from Westchester County in New York. A fellow New Yorker.

These were the days before cell phones, so I really did not have a way to reach out to her unless I ran into her, but I knew what car she drove: a sporty red Mazda X, which was easy to spot in the Killington parking lot. I would often drop her a note leaving it under the windshield wiper. I asked her to meet me one morning early at Superstar chair for some runs. We both showed up, but the weather was cold, icy, and rainy. We took one run, and it was crazy bad. We decided to quit. I wanted to spend time with her, so I suggested we take a drive to Lake Champlain in Burlington, Vermont a two-hour drive. She agreed and off we went with me playing hooky from work.

We talked the entire time there and got to know one another better. She grew up in Yorktown, New York, which was about an hour from Poughkeepsie. She came from a good Catholic family. We had many things in common.

I drove to Burlington and headed to Lake Champlain. The sun came out just as we parked at the edge of the lake, and it was beautiful. I immediately felt like I had met someone that I could see myself with going forward. The day ended with us going for pizza in Pittsford. It was a great date, and I knew I wanted more.

We continued to see each other, and I communicated often via my car notes, which often made me feel like I was stalking her. One night we went out dancing at the Wobbly Barn and Pickle Barrel. She could really dance. We skied together as often as possible. Talking with her was easy and we shared the same interests, like food and skiing. She was not a golfer, but willing to learn.

She was in hot pursuit by at least one other guy from her area in New York. I was aware of him and did my best to win her over. I knew I did not want to play the field, so after a couple of months, I told her I loved her. It was spring, and we were laying alongside Kent Pond in Killington on a blanket, and I told her for the first time. She said she was falling in love as well, but she had other suitors and insisted that if we were to pursue this love affair, I would have to act on my separation and finalize the divorce.

We had a profoundly serious discussion about our future that included a conversation about having children of our own. I had a strong feeling that my two girls were enough for me and amazingly she felt that she did not want kids either. She was 32 years old and her window to have any was shrinking fast. She loved her life, which included lots of vacations, skiing and beaching, and her freedom. I was sold on her.

I immediately went to work to finalize the divorce. I had written our stipulation and presented it to the judge in Rutland Court. I did not have a lawyer and represented myself. The judge was floored that we both could agree on all points and quickly granted the divorce decree. He commented to the lawyers and others in the room, "There is a lesson here for all of you. A divorce can be done without fighting and lawyers." It made me happy in many ways.

I had moved into my condominium, and Teri started to stay with me when she was at Killington. I so looked forward to her coming up and our sex life was highly active. When the ski season ended our relationship did not. I would travel down to New York to her condominium in Peekskill. It was a large, one bedroom that she had bought on her own a few years prior. She was an RN at Westchester Medical Center in the pediatric dept. and had a lot of flexibility in her scheduling that allowed her to create long stretches of time off. She would come and stay with me when she could.

She had rented an apartment in Newport Beach, Rhode Island that summer with some of her close girlfriends, so she and I would often go down there for weekends. She looked just like the actor Judith Light and would often get mistaken for her. I had truly landed on my feet. I remember asking her to marry me while laying on a beach in Newport. I did not think I would ever experience love again. She said yes, so our fairy tale romance would continue.

In 1991, I was the Division Controller for Killington Ski Resort when I was approached by a hospitality recruiter by the name of Jacque Pelletier. I knew him through the various National Ski Areas Association (NSAA) trade shows. He always thought that my resume was strong and that I could continue to grow in the industry. I was riding a high at Killington and doing well.

One day he called me and said that he had a position he was looking to fill. It was an opening for Treasurer and Director of Base Operations at Loon Mountain in New Hampshire, about an hour and a half from Killington. "Do you have any interest?" I asked him to let me check it out, and after doing so, I told him to submit my resume.

I met with Sam Adams, who was the son of Sherman Adams, who was the famous Chief of State to President Dwight Eisenhower back in the fifties. He had gotten in trouble and was forced to resign for taking an animal coat for free.

Sam was a mineralogist in the Colorado region. He had just taken over as president of Loon in a hostile takeover move and then fired Phil Gravink, who had been the long-time president. Loon was in the process of obtaining permission from the United States Forest Service for growth in the South Mountain area. It was a long and tedious process, and after 10 years they still did not have approvals. Gravink had tried his best but was the sacrificial lamb; the board put Sam Adams in as president. I was going to report to him as Corporate Treasurer and Director of Base Operations. The position was like what I was doing at Killington, but there were more growth opportunities at Loon. I accepted the position and a raise to $65,000 per year, which was about $15,000 more than what I was making at Killington.

I had recently started to date my future wife, Teri Cook, before I had left Killington. I had fallen deeply in love with Teri and saw a future with her. I was overjoyed when she said she would move with me. She was going to remain a nurse and commute back to her job in Westchester County as a registered nurse. We moved in together in a townhome in Lincoln, New Hampshire. Although I was moving away from my daughters, I felt that I could still make co-parenting work. Luckily, I had the cooperation of my ex-wife Lorraine who would meet me on the border of Vermont and New Hampshire when it was my turn to take the kids.

I began my new position with great anticipation and excitement. One of my key responsibilities was to prepare the financial reports for the board of directors. I had not been doing that for Killington as that was Marty Wilson's job. Sam was very particular with how he wanted me to write the financial results each month. He was fanatical about it. I would do it the way he said, but it was never good enough.

My controller was a woman by the name of Nancy Donahue and the general manager was the former treasurer, Mike Somma. I was hoping that I was going to be able to improve Loon's software systems and began to review their financial software, which was not particularly old, but it did not have the ability to close out the profits and losses weekly, which I wanted to do to improve financial results. I was accustomed to doing it at Killington and strongly believed that monitoring our revenue and expenses weekly would produce higher profits, so I convinced Sam to make the change.

The resort was also using the typical old lift ticket system with paper tickets attached to a wicket. I had been introduced to the ski data radio frequency program at one of the NSAA conventions. No one else in New England was using it and I saw Loon being on the forefront of innovation by installing it.

Those two software enhancements were implemented for the winter of 1992-93. There is no question that I was pushing the staff and the departments to work hard to make these new installations work properly. I needed buy-in from the controller Nancy, and I do not think she ever really liked that we were changing the financial software. In time, over the winter we were able to start to make it work the way it was intended, but I was making enemies along the way.

The ticketing system was another story. Although in concept it should have worked, it was not acclimating well to the temperatures in New England, which could reach 30 degrees below zero. We were having problems with the radio frequency gun receiving the signal from the pass. Although this technology is used at ski resorts all over today, back in those days, skiers were not accustomed to this type of entry to lifts. It broke down often and more than once I was called into the president's office to justify this purchase. I knew I was not making him happy, but we had set out on a path, and we could not turn back. I was anxiously waiting for the end of the season to get out of the hot water I was in and get the system working properly. during the I was also anxious because I was getting married.

Wedding Bells

Teri and I got married the weekend of March 27th, 1993. We were to get married on the deck at the lodge at the top of Loon. All our friends and family were invited. Unfortunately, Teri had torn her ACL/MCL six weeks earlier at Sunday River, no thanks to me. We were getting off a lift and my ski caught the top of hers and I dragged her ski and leg with me when we got off and boom, and they both tore. She had the operation, and we were hopeful at the wedding she could get around. It would turn out that she was able to get out of the cast the day before the wedding.

The week of the wedding was glorious with blue skies and temperatures rising from the low sixties to seventy-five on the Saturday of the wedding. Many friends and family came up during the days before, so we had a lot of fun skiing in bluebird warm days. Unfortunately, Teri was still in the cast and missed a great ski week.

I drove to the mountain on my wedding day and Mike Somma, the general manager, was excited to see me as I walked toward the office building. The ticket lines were huge thanks to the amazing weather. I immediately started selling tickets for cash out front to help. The day was off to an interesting start.

All kinds of cool things happened at the wedding. We played music and danced in the middle of the ceremony, which flipped my parents out. As we left the deck, we were given a ski pole salute that we had to walk through. Because of Teri's knee surgery, we took a ride down from the top in a toboggan led by a ski patroller, who was dressed in a tuxedo. On the way down, we were pelted by snowballs, which for some reason the skiers thought would be a good idea. We rode by the main party deck at the base lodge to the cheers of hundreds. It was quite fun.

The wedding was broadcast live on a major radio station in New Hampshire. It was part of a weekend sales pitch to drive customers to the resort that the marketing manager thought would be fun. One of our wedding guests from New York was driving along listening to the station when our wedding came on the air. They were blown away. They had decided to skip the wedding and just come to the reception, but they missed quite the event. It was hard to believe that we had the luck of having our wedding at the top of a mountain, on a deck overlooking the White Mountains on a 75-degree sunny day.

The full day was beautiful and memorable. We held our reception at the Governor's Lodge that evening with 150 friends and family in attendance, and it was a beautiful occasion. Teri was able to dance with her new knee brace and we topped off the night by doing our infamous karaoke version of "I Got You Babe" by Sonny and Cher. It just might be one of the worst renditions ever. It was a great party. I had married the women of my dreams.

However, the season did not turn out great financially and the board was looking to make some expense reductions. I was called into the president's office and found myself being let go by Sam Adams one morning right before we were scheduled to go on our honeymoon, which we were packed to do. I can remember going home and waking Teri up and telling her I was being let go. We both shed tears, but at the same time I think I had realized earlier that I was not a good mix with that type of management culture. I was not good at being complacent and I was always looking to do different things in the hopes that it would improve operations. This was a resort that was living in the dark ages and living in the glory of their past. It was not a good match and although I was out of a job, I believed in myself and that something would come up, so off we went on our honeymoon to Aruba. I truly had found the love of my life in Teri. We were compatible in many ways. We discussed my options, which included getting out of the ski industry.

I knew only one thing, which is that I had an amazing wife and life partner in Teri. One afternoon I came back into our hotel room in Barbados and saw the phone red light blinking. I picked up the phone and listened to a message that would change my life. It was Les Otten, who was the owner of Sunday River Ski Resort in Maine. He had heard about me being available through Marty Wilson, who was his good friend and my former Killington boss. He said he had a position open as Vice President of Finance at Sunday River and suggested that when I get back to reach out to him. I had gotten to know Les in the late eighties when he was expanding Sunday River and developing real estate. Killington had transferred him to run Sunday River as general manager and then eventually SKI LTD. sold it to him for $900,000. Les remained good friends with Marty Wilson, who was the controller of SKI Ltd. and to whom I reported. I can remember being in Marty's office on Saturday afternoons and he would often call Marty and tell us his joke of the week. He was a great joke teller. I had never met him face-to-face, but I had heard a lot about him.

Our first in-person meeting together was not at Sunday River, but at Wildcat Mountain in New Hampshire, which is within an hour of Sunday River and at the time was recognized as a diamond in the rough. Les told me that his objective going forward was to investigate the purchase of other ski resorts in New England, and Wildcat was his first target. He offered me a huge pay raise to be part of his team to help with these acquisitions. It was very flattering, and I was struck by his youthfulness and good looks., It only took me a minute to accept his offer.

The first week I was on the job, the director of base operations resigned, and Les approached me about taking on that position as well. I had filled that role at Loon and Killington, so it was not something I was uncomfortable doing. I said sure, but he never said, "I will pay you more money." Within a short timeframe I had not only gotten a wonderful job at a great and upcoming company, but I had hooked up with a true ski pioneer and visionary. Our future was bright together.

Les and I worked well together. We both liked the Yankees, which did not hurt our relationship. He trusted me, and I trusted him. He was tough to work for and had a reputation for being temperamental, but I quickly learned how to deal with it. We grew the company quickly and with it my role grew as well. He was busy chasing other ski resorts to buy and because of it, I eventually would reach the pinnacle of the ski industry.

Once I accepted the position at Sunday River, Teri and I moved to Bethel, Maine. I immediately felt I belonged at the resort. I experienced a welcoming staff who loved their jobs. I am not sure if Les knew in advance of my arrival that his director of base operations would be leaving, but the guy left days after I started. Les knew I ran base ops at both Loon and Killington and asked me if I would take it over. Of course, I said yes, but I did not get offered any more money, which was very typical in the ski industry. Les wanted to upgrade some base facilities and I was asked to head the summer projects. We built new decks, road signage, and upgraded the restaurant and bars at both Barker and South Ridge lodges. I named one of the new bars, "Foggy Googles," hence, the name of this book. I hired a good friend from Loon, Don Lawton, as general contractor. He did excellent work, and the projects went well.

Teri accepted a position as the RN in charge of the base area ski patrol clinic. We worked near each other, and it was fun. We would come home and swap war stories. She was a good clinical manager and started the first drug testing process for ski area employment applicants in the country. I used to laugh upon seeing a potential employee walk up the staircase, read the sign saying they would be drug tested, and watch them turn around and leave and never complete the application.

We wound up renting a beautiful townhouse way up on a mountainside on Powder Ridge Mountain, only a few miles from the resort. I was now making $85k per year. Within a short stretch of one month, I found myself at an amazing, growing ski resort. It was a vast improvement over my Loon Mountain experience.

We were settling in nicely and when an opportunity came up to buy one of my fellow senior manager's home, and we jumped all over it. It was on Songo Pond, just outside of Bethel proper. We loved the thought of living on the nearby lake (we were across the road) and soon after bought a small parcel of land right on the water that we renovated to include a little boat house for storage and a dock area. Of course, I had to have a speedboat, so I found one to purchase. Life was good, but about to change.

My youngest daughter, Lindsay, decided to attend Gould Academy and would be moving in with Teri and me. I was excited that she wanted to live with us, and she moved in prior to her freshman year. Teri had not spent that much consistent time with her, so there would be an adjustment needed on everyone's part. I was working a lot and missed some of the interaction with my daughters, but like most teenagers, Lindsay was not easy to effect change on. She had a temper and mixed with my temper and with Teri in the background getting mad at me because of her, it got ugly at times.

For the first time in our marriage, Teri was not happy. She and Lindsay clashed. Lindsay was not a very neat person and her room looked like a bomb hit it. She was not always respectful to Teri, which was typical of a teenager. Teri was only her stepmother and I do not think they were compatible. It made for a difficult four years as I loved them both dearly and often felt split or could see both sides. The good news is that when Lindsay got married, she pulled Teri aside and told her how much she loved her and appreciated all she did for her and for putting up with her while at Gould Academy. It was very touching, and they have been remarkably close ever since.

Life has a funny way of acting itself out, but at the end of the day, love guides our actions. It took me awhile to realize how important family really is towards my mental and physical well-being, but now that I have and as I age, I appreciate family even more. I was blessed when Lindsay and her family moved to Utah from Boston in 2018. I miss my oldest daughter Erin and her husband Greg, who are still back east in the Boston area. My parents have passed, but not some great memories of two beautiful people.

For the most part, our Maine journey was wonderful. Mainers are simply good people. However, there was a time when I got a speeding ticket driving to work one morning. I was speeding, so I deserved the ticket. The police officer did not say much and was nice—or so I thought. I did not mention it to Lindsay as it was not a big deal. One night she came back home telling us how a police officer was with her and a group of her friends, bragging how he had given me a ticket. He knew I was someone important at Sunday River and thought it was cool. He did not know that Lindsay was my daughter. She came home and told me the story laughing hysterically.

"Teri is cooking tonight." Those words, when spoken to friends or family bring immediate joy to them and me. We are both foodies and love good, diverse types of food and drink. When we first met, she won me over with her warm heart, personality, looks, and her abilities as a chef.

For almost 30 years, I have been treated daily to some of the most amazing five-star dinners. Thank God for my daily morning walks with our dogs and being active in sports, which helps me keep my weight in check. She loves being in her kitchen and can spend the day puttering around, chopping veggies, or making something delicious. She grew up in a mixed nationality family, but her mother was primarily Italian, and it rubbed off. I just love her pasta meat sauce and have never tasted better, except for my Bolognese sauce. I have often thought that we should open a home cooked, family style restaurant. She has always rejected the idea.

I settled in quickly and luckily had an amazing staff that I could depend on, including three great guys. Jim Largesse, who oversaw food and beverage and Steve Perry, who oversaw building maintenance and had been at Sunday River for a while. I was also in charge of the ski school, which was headed up by Bob Harkins, who at one point had been on the U.S. ski team. I had a wonderful team on the base operations side. I was also always fortunate to have great admins to help me along. I miss all those people.

Our accounting and IT staff was led by Dave Langlois. He had developed his own ticketing system and had managed to develop software for a weekly close to the profit-and-loss statement so that management could make immediate decisions based on the prior week's performance. He was a veteran ski resort guy and very dependable, but he did not always agree with everything I wanted to do or to change. He would fight back, and if it made more sense, than we did it his way.

Our acquisition growth in the initial years was under a company called LBO Holdings Inc. Les asked me to see what I thought about the financials of the resort companies and try to determine if it would be a good purchase. We worked extremely hard with the owners who were older. At the end of the day, we could not strike a deal with Wildcat.

During this effort, we had also reached out to Phil Gravink, who, after Loon, had become the president of Attitash Resort, just outside of Cranmore, New Hampshire. Their board was interested in selling the resort. We had immediate interest in buying them as there was significant growth potential, which included a new area called Bear Mountain. We would also pursue approvals to build a "Grand Summit" quarter-share hotel, like the two built at Sunday River, which had proven to be phenomenally successful. Terrain expansion was just in the beginning phases of discussion, and it was obvious with Les's background it was something that we could accomplish. We hired Carl Spangler, who had been the Vice President of Development for Killington. He led the charge to get Bear Mountain permitted and approved and we moved forward with the purchase. Les had his second ski resort and we were optimistic about our future.

We worked closely with Bank of Boston and one of their vice presidents of the ski portfolios named Brooks Hoffman. Brooks also was the banker for Loon Mountain, so I had met him previously, and we had spent time together over the time I was at Loon. In fact, one funny story was the night we out went out to a local bar called the Woodstock Inn when it was karaoke night. Brooks got on stage as did Teri and me as a singing duo. The next day, I got a phone call from the woman who was the owner who witnessed our performances. She said, "Brooks the banker, was by far the best karaoke singer we've ever had here." He had sung an amazing rendition of Michael Jackson's "Thriller", including dancing. Surprisingly, she then went on to say, "And Teri and you were probably the worst we've ever had." We had sung a rendition of "I Got You Babe" by Sonny and Cher. We committed at that time to get better at singing the song and did it at our wedding.

We set our sights on more acquisitions and found out that Sugarbush Resort in Warren, Vermont was for sale. Sugarbush had a great reputation as one of the premiere New England ski resorts and had a great history. There were two mountain areas that comprised Sugarbush, called Sugarbush North and Mt. Ellen, or South; however, they were not connected via any lift system. Les saw the potential of connecting the two mountains via an interconnect and help grow skier days. Once again, the opportunity to build another "Grand Summit" type quarter-share hotel was also a strong possibility but would meet tougher obstacles in environmentally sensitive Vermont.

We were able to hire Alan Wilson, who was formerly Division Controller of Killington prior to me, and then CFO of Bear Mountain in California. SKI Ltd. had purchased it years earlier and had completed major improvements to the resort in the late 1980s. Alan was the perfect guy. He had hired me into the ski industry in 1983 as internal auditor for Killington. He and I were good friends and went way back, including vacations to Martha's Vineyard. We added Rich McGarry from Killington, as his general manager, creating an extraordinarily strong management team.

Once again, we needed to refinance our main line of credit, so Bank of Boston was called upon. The bank saw the potential we had in our growing brand of ski resorts, which included quarter-share hotels, mountain expansion with new terrain, and new or upgraded lifts. With the addition of Attitash and Sugarbush to the Sunday River family, we were riding high and were threatening to overtake SKI LTD. in total skier days per season.

It was an exciting time for LBO Holdings and the need for faster transportation became a necessity. Les decided a twin-engine turbo prop plane would help us out, so we hired a pilot, Dan Bilodeau, and leased a plane. We were flying high, literally, and opportunities were coming in from every direction. We were most fortunate that many staff members from Sunday River took advantage of growth opportunities and assumed more responsibility. When we advertised for specific management jobs, we were presented with many credible options as others were excited about the prospects of joining a growing company, especially in the ski industry.

Sugarbush was a resort with immense potential, and we were able to capitalize on it. We received approval for the interconnecting gondola and work began immediately. We also created a season pass that allowed buyers to ski Sunday River, Attitash, and Sugarbush on one pass. It was an immediate hit on the east coast and was truly the forerunner of today's Epic and Ikon passes. The company was starting to develop and grow as Les envisioned. I could not believe my good fortune. In a matter of three years, I had not only recovered from the Loon fiasco, but I prospered. At the same time, my daughter Erin was attending Northeastern University in Boston and Lindsay, a prep school in Bethel and with the money rolling in from my raises, what was once something that seemed impossible to fund turned out to be easy.

Life was going well, and I was remarkably busy. Teri and I were experiencing life with my daughter Lindsay living with us. Teri and I had been married only one year and this became our first true test as a couple. Teri had issues with Lindsay, as she saw things differently than us, as expected from a teenager. They were left together more than I would have preferred as I was travelling quite a bit to both the new resorts and to Boston or New York city for financing needs.

I remember one fall morning leaving my house, driving to the airport in Bethel, flying down to Boston in our twin-engine plane, taking the water taxi, and walking from the pier to the Financial District in one hour and 15 minutes. Les's and my time were precious, and the demands to fund our acquisitions were dizzying. As I became busier in acquisitions, I was feeling more pressure to perform my normal functions, as I was still running base operations at Sunday River as well as being Vice President of Finance. I was fortunate to have hired some key individuals, including Chip Vicary, Chris Lavek, Dan Kashman, and Peter Mutty to take on various accounting or finance positions.

I had a great staff, but I must admit I pushed them hard at times. I would describe my management style as a mix of being a team builder and someone that needed to be demanding on individuals at times. I often thought that I was not the person I strived to be as a manager. I did not really like the person I had to become to make my point. But I still did it, as I could not find a way to change my behavior. I have been trying for years to be the best person I can be, but my toughness has occasionally come up and bit me on the ass from time to time over the last 35 years. I had certain expectations from my staff, which in my mind were simple. An employee is being paid to do an EXCELLENT job and one should be doing just that. When this was not being met, I was not afraid of saying so and acting. Some people do not like being called out on realities or their deficiencies, so it was a tricky situation for me at times.

I have struggled to be a different type of leader, which is one I can be proud of, but I have not always been successful. I like to blame it on being a former New Yorker with the old "You need to be tough to survive in New York" mentality. I am certainly a type A personality, which has gotten me far in life, but hopefully not because I have steamrolled people. I would like to believe that many people that have worked for me over the years would have good things to say about me as their boss. I suppose it never hurts to have these positive beliefs, but if not true, then I will still go to my death bed knowing that I never intentionally tried to hurt someone. It just is not in my DNA.

My desire was to change and be that perfect boss, someone who is a gentle and understanding person. I now like to believe that being Cami full time and presenting myself as a female has softened me.

The only way I could make the extra work and my demands up to my key staff was to give them healthy salary increases during their annual review process. In retrospect, it almost looks like I was buying them and maybe to some degree I was, but I was also being pushed hard by Les, who was a very demanding and temperamental boss.

I could handle Les's management style as being a former New Yorker toughened me. When he started yelling at me, I would just leave his office and tell him to see me when he calmed down. He always would come in and apologize, but he still managed to strongly re-emphasize his point or needs. It was a quasi-win for me, but I always respected his final opinions and accomplished what he wanted. I would label myself a "good soldier."

I had the ability to work well with our vendors, especially our bankers, including Brooks Hoffman at Bank of Boston, who, in the first years of our growth, was a key player. We became friends and when he was often frustrated with Les's demands, I could easily identify with him and to some degree, agreed with him, but kept him moving towards the end game. We were being recognized as the movers and shakers in the ski industry, with our only competition developing out west by Vail Resorts, owned by Apollo Group, an investment fund out of New York City and George Gillett's Booth Creek Holdings.

I was living a life and having a career that I would have never expected and loving every moment.

In 1996 following the acquisition of Sugarbush, we set our targets on the next opportunity out there which would enable us to become the east coast's largest ski resort company. We would make a run at SKI Ltd., the owner of Killington where both Les and I started our careers. We believed it would be available at the right purchase price. Both Pres Smith, who was CEO and Marty Wilson, who was CFO, were good friends of ours. But business is business, and we needed to produce our best offer.

SKI had purchased Waterville Valley in New Hampshire and Sugarloaf Mountain in Maine over the past few years. They had owned for many years Mount Snow in Vermont, as well as the original Killington flagship resort. After some initial back and forth, we made a final offer of $104 million that was accepted. It would be bittersweet for all of us and certainly a case of what goes around, comes around. I had started working under Marty Wilson as an internal auditor in 1983. He remained my boss for years and I believe was one of the most influential individuals in my life that I have ever met. He was my mentor. Marty had suffered from polio from when he was a young kid and walked with a very noticeable limp. Despite his handicap, it never stopped him from doing anything, including skiing, and eventually sailing around the world with his amazing wife, Marge.

Pres would retire and get a payout worth about $11 million for his part ownership of SKI LTD, which had been diluted when going public years earlier. It has been well documented how Pres started Killington from scratch in the early 1950s. He had an ambitious dream to build a world-class ski resort in Vermont and he made it happen. It grew to be one of the largest ski resorts in the country and surpassed over 1.1 million skier days while I was controller. It struck me that $11 million after all that time, some 50 years, just did not seem like enough.

Pres was quite the businessperson. He was very shrewd, aloof, and kept to himself. He had strong opinions, including his extreme dislike of Vermont governors, like the environmentally sensitive Madeline Kuehn. I recall one day in the Lodging Center where he was hosting her and her environmental cohorts from the Environmental Commission. They were there to discuss the proposed ski connection between Pico and Killington and water issues. He stopped them as they were walking up the stairs, turned to the Governor, and said directly, "I don't know why I am treating you so nice, I really don't like you." He had a bit of a strange edge, but I was always in awe of what he built.

Pres could also have a great sense of humor. Back in my early crossdressing days, I remember one Halloween I went dressed with one side of me as a man and the other side as a woman, requiring me to shave half of a mustache that I had for years. It was a great costume because, depending on what side you were looking at, it was remarkably different, yet realistic. I went to work in the costume, and later that afternoon when Pres walked out of his office, he saw me, and he started to stare at me on the female side (he always was a heartbreaker), but when I turned to the male side, he looked confused. He quickly realized it was a costume and started laughing. He came up to me to look closer and said, "That's good, really good."

The purchase of SKI Ltd. was important for our growing company. The purchase required us to float two subordinated bonds, one for $120 million and the other for $39 million. Bear Stearns underwrote the deal. It was our first major foray into the Wall Street bank scene. It was crazy to think that we were growing so fast and that I was helping to acquire financing to make it happen from Wall Street banks. It required many long days in putting together the prospectus, which would explain our company, the purchase of SKI Ltd., and expansion plans. It was long days often spent in an office in some skyscraper in NYC, eating take out and working into the wee hours. We also had to make presentations to financial advisors for potential bond purchases.

On June 25, 1996, we closed on the bonds and had the financing required to complete the purchase of Killington. It was a bittersweet closing as Pres, Marty, Frank Urso, Killington's corporate attorney well as my longtime friend and personal attorney and coworker while at Killington, Joe Sargeant, Chris Howard, Les and I met in NYC to sign the paperwork, which there was a lot of. We toasted champagne at the end. Everyone knew the new guard was taking over at Killington and changes would be likely. Pres's baby would not be the same, but I was happy for all of them to be cashing out. I found it ironic that I would now be overseeing Marty, so we created a position for him to stay on, which was more for show then anything and I never really had to ask him to do anything. I continued to view him as my mentor, but I do not think he ever viewed me as his superior.

We had some issues in making the deal happen. The Department of Justice ruled that we would be creating a monopoly by buying SKI and were violating anti-trust laws by controlling so many eastern resorts. Early that year, I helped purchase Cranmore Ski Resort in New Hampshire for a few million dollars. SKI had purchased Sugarloaf in Maine and Waterville Valley in New Hampshire over the past couple of years as well. In total, we would own eight resorts in New England. After much negotiation by our Chief Counsel Chris Howard, the DOJ ruled against us and we wound up having to sell off Cranmore and Waterville Valley, leaving us with Sunday River, Attitash, Sugarbush, Mt. Snow, Sugarloaf, and Killington, which easily ranked us as the largest in the east in terms of skier days. We were getting major attention in the ski media, and Les Otten was a rising star in the industry. I was just one of the people behind him that was helping to make things happen. We were still looking to add more ski resorts, so what could be better than a resort right in my and LBO's backyard in New York State?

Hunter Mountain Ski Resort was and still is a legendary resort in New York. When I was a firefighter, we use to participate in the annual firefighter's ski race at Hunter Mountain in New York's Catskill Mountains. Imagine five guys holding on to a 100-foot length of firehose and going through gates. It was hard to do and very funny to watch, especially if you were in the rear. It was a good reason to party all day and I remember the fun we all had all day long.

Les knew the founders of Hunter Mountain, Orville and Izzy Slutzsky, through the ski industry, and Les set his sights on buying it. Mike Krongel had joined us and served as our expansion scout and representative. He was a friend of Les's from his college days, and he had a background in real estate, which was proving to be helpful.

Mike had contacted Orville and Izzy about a potential acquisition. Their sons, Paul and David, had gotten involved in the business years prior as both Izzy and Orville were getting on in years, being in their mid-seventies. They were really from the old school. Orville was the general manager and Izzy was the snowmaking wizard, having been recognized in the ski industry as one of the founders of the snowmaking process. Hunter was known for their snowmaking in those days as they would take big hits with rain in the middle of the winter and needed to rebound quickly. That they did. We saw Hunter as a great entry into the New York market, which we could leverage to get skiers to our New England resorts using our popular joint resort season pass.

We hired a great real estate manager in Mike Meyers, who was brought in to obtain permits and handle construction of the Grand Hotels at Attitash and Sugarbush. Mike was out of Boston and was a true Bostonian, with the accent to prove it. He was street smart, as well as college educated. He immediately took over construction of the Attitash hotel and jumped into the fray at Sugarbush to try to get the permits needed to start construction. He was under a lot of pressure as Les pushed him hard.

We sent Mike to Hunter to stay and understand the real estate potential. We would often fly down for a day in our twin engine and land at a grass strip that also served as a cow pasture. Before attempting to land, our pilot, Dan, would circle the field to check to see if it were clear of cows. One day he was attempting to land to pick Mike and me up and he circled and decided to land. Little did he or we realize that walking up the dirt road was a herd of cows being guided by a guy on horseback (see picture below). It might have been the local airstrip, but this was their pasture, and they were going in and no plane was going to stop them. Mike and I panicked, running out into the strip/field and trying to get Dan's attention to not land. The option to have the cows go elsewhere seemed impossible as they were walking into the field. Luckily, Dan noticed the cows at the last moment and aborted the landing.

Les had an immediate connection to Orville and Izzy. They were also Jewish, and that kindred spirit went a long way. They liked all of us and it was always enjoyable to talk to them. A lot of time was spent telling us how things were in the old days. One day Les and I flew down and Izzy picked us up at the airport. Instead of them taking us to the resort, we went on a little side excursion to the local cemetery. We pulled in and Orville and Izzy proudly directed us to a specific location. Izzy stopped the car and Orville proudly said, "This is where we will be buried." Les and I were surprised to be there. You do not get to see that kind of openness too often. Although in retrospect it is funny, at the time it was their way of saying that they trusted us. They wanted us to be the buyers if it was to be sold.

It was always a trip driving with Izzy. The rear bumper of his Cadillac was prolific with dents and scratches from the numerous times he just backed up without looking and hit something. I remember him blowing through a stop sign on the way to the airport with Les and I in the backseat. Orville, Les, and I all yelled "Izzy, stop sign," which he blew through. Izzy's response was, "That stop sign shouldn't have been there anyway."

The sons, David and Paul, were good businesspeople and were behind the scenes taking over the reins. Orville still had an office just off the main cafeteria and conveniently next to the cash room, which was managed by Edith, Orville's wife of 50 years or so. His office was classic with some thirty closed circuit TV screens showing the video feed from various places at the resort. He could see it all. Once you got into the office you had to be prepared to hear stories (again) and to stay awhile.

I delved into their financial records, which were produced by his long-time accountant and friend in NYC. They were spotty at best. Not a lot of detail on departmental performance and trying to make heads or tails of the financials was hit and miss. We did know their skier day count and we could always use that as a basis to run some projections. Something was not really adding up and I suspected that perhaps a lot of cash was not making it to the bank nor the books. It was a family business and was still being run as such. Cash is king. We casually would bring it up, but they never indicated that it was the case. We had to base our decision on what we thought the revenues should be based on skier days.

Unfortunately for them, there was a formula that we and other resort companies were using to value resorts for sale, which was a multiple of EBITDA, which stands for earnings before interest, taxes, depreciation, and amortization. In other words, it was available cash flow at the end of a year. We would then multiply that number times the going rate at the time for resorts of around ten times to generate the price it was worth. By not reporting all revenue received, a resort was hurting itself as upon a sale, every dollar not reported would be worth $10. Our valuation came in at $17.5 million dollars and that was our offer. They expected it to be higher, I closer to $30 million. We explained our logic and I believe that David and Paul, the sons, could see that our offer would be like others and wanted to work with us. We were getting closer, but Orville and Izzy were still working every day and loved it. I would say that Orville's toughest job was to collect the cash from the vending machines scattered throughout the base lodge. There is that magic word again: cash.

Skiers of Hunter loved seeing Orville and Izzy floating around the base lodge. They were Hunter Mountain. This was their baby and to sell it, at any price, would be difficult. After months of trying to get a deal done, we all found ourselves at the National Ski Area Association's annual meeting in Marco Island. Our wives were also with us. I had planned to catch up with Orville and see if we could close the deal while there.

Orville always liked me. Once he even said to me, "You know, you'd make a good Jew." I took that as a real compliment. During the convention, I was in my room getting ready for a night event with Teri when the phone rang. It was Orville. He asked me to please come up to his room and to please bring Teri. An unusual request, but up we went. He welcomed us in and told us to "sit on the bed" as he wanted to tell us something. In an emotional moment that I will never forget he said, "Tommy, if I sell this resort to you guys, I'm going die and I don't want to die." He would not do it and no amount of money was going to change his mind. There was nothing more for me to do. I was not about to challenge him and keep selling the idea. I called Les and told him what he said. He tried to get me to talk to him, but I knew No meant No. I suggested to Les that he talk to him. I'm not sure if he ever did, but I know that was the last time I ever discussed buying their resort.

The resort finally sold in 2015, 18 years later, for $36.5 million. Orville knew he could get more then we offered and eventually they did. He lived till 2013 and died at the age of ninety-six, so clearly not selling the resort kept him alive. Some things were meant to be and buying Hunter was not one of them. Les had bigger ideas and since we were the largest in the east, the west seemed a natural place to head.

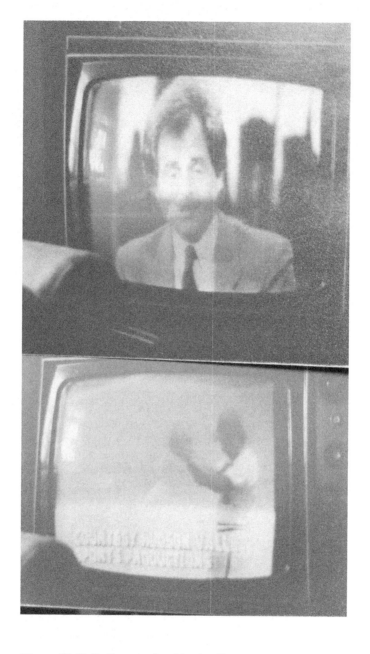

Warner Wolf- "Let's go to the videotape"

Rich Fishwick and I after fighting a fire on a frosty winter day, 1982

Killington Ski Trip, 2017

My Grand Prix that, during a hurricane, I crashed into a falling tree

Marching down Main Street in Park City in the 4th of July parade, 2021

Teri and I in Mexico, 2018

Rob and Londa's house in Vermont before the fire

This photo changed my life

Our first big date, Teri's brother's wedding, 1991

The Silver Bullet

In the summer of 1993, amidst all the energy our company was putting into our potential acquisition of Attitash Ski Resort in New Hampshire, Les Otten, who solely owned Sunday River, envisioned a ski train that would connect the mountain with Auburn, Portland and Boston (through a Portland to Boston passenger rail line that never materialized until 2001 in the form of the Amtrak Downeaster).

It was to be part of a larger commercial and residential project that was proposed by Heinie Merrill and Grant Wilson, partners in the development of the Sunday River Brewery, and Les. As first introduced, the plan envisioned a $25 million commercial development within the former mill/industrial area lying within thirty-six acres between the railroad and Androscoggin River and bordered on the west by Route 2, and on the east by Route 26.

Les appointed Carl Spangler to head the ski train effort and get the necessary approvals, which was his specialty. That summer, a set of seven heritage cars were purchased from the Indiana Railroad, and the St. Lawrence and Atlantic Railroad was hired to operate the train. Buses were also purchased from Chicago Transit Authority to carry skiers from the station in Bethel to the mountain.

As Vice President of Base Operations, I was asked to head up the operations of the train while in the station, including the food and beverage operations and coordinating the bus operation. Jeff Frost, a dynamic employee who headed up ski events for the resort, was appointed as the Train Operations Manager. He worked tirelessly to get the train up and running as it was an older train and needed lots of work. I recall many a cold evening on my way home I would stop and see Jeff under the train, soldering something or repairing a hose line. It was a crazy, dizzying time and the excitement for the inaugural train ride was a marketing marvel as only Les Otten could do.

The Silver Bullet Express was also known as the Sunday River Ski Train and was sponsored by Coors Light. The train left Portland at 6:45 a.m., arriving in Bethel at 8:45 am where passengers transferred to buses which would take them to the mountain. The return trip would depart Bethel at 5:15 p.m. Amenities included a dining car, parlor car, and a retrofitted boxcar for carrying skis and snowboards. It operated from 1993 until 1996.

On Christmas Eve 1993, I was headed out to dinner with Teri and my daughter Lindsay. We stopped at the train as it was the first night it was to open for dinner in the dining car. As usual, Jeff was busy running around, and unfortunately, the crowd was much larger than expected and the food team was understaffed. As always, I jumped in to help in whatever way I could and so did Teri and Lindsay. We bussed tables, served food, and seated patrons and it turned out to be a fun experience, although not the dining experience we had anticipated.

Operating the ski train turned out to be a difficult challenge as the weather during the winter in Maine could get very cold and we often had to deal with freezing pipes and lines. It also was a much longer time experience for those using the train to get to and from the mountain. Our effort got favorable press reviews, but at the end of the day was a money loser and eventually ended in a slow death.

In early 1997, Les sent Mike Krongel, our real estate representative, to check out a small but developable resort in Park City, Utah called Wolf Mountain, formerly Park West. For years, this resort struggled in the shadows of nearby Park City Mountain Resort and Deer Valley. It had some incredible ski terrain and the current owners, Kenny Griswold and Mike Baker, were trying to piece together more land to expand towards the PCMR property. It was only doing about 75,000 skier days per season, so it had plenty of room to grow. It logistically was only 35 minutes from the Salt Lake City Airport, and it would be our perfect segue to western resorts. Les was overly excited about this resort. It did not have any reliable financial history to base a decision on, it just had the potential to be huge.

I went out in May 1997 after they had closed for the year. I recall my reaction to pulling up to the base lodge in a dirt, dusty parking lot. I was in shock, wondering what did Les saw in the place. I met Kenny, one of the owners, in his office and he was a very gregarious guy. He explained the expansion plans on a land map. Being a money guy, my thought was "this is going to take a lot of money." I was introduced to Steve Huntsberger, the food and beverage manager, who took me on a groomer for a ride to the top of Lookout Ridge. There was a top lodge, which was our destination. We walked in and my mouth dropped open. It was a mess. Furniture all over. Dusty and dirty. I was not used to seeing this type of disarray. I did as much research that I could and reported back to Les. I told him that I did not have the same attraction to the place as he did, in fact, my exact words were "It's a dump." He pulled out his topo map with a depiction of potential mountain areas and lifts. He said, "It will be the largest ski resort in Utah when built out." It turns out, he was right. He was like a kid in a candy store. He had built Sunday River from scratch and saw the opportunity to do it again at Wolf. Nothing I could say was going to change his desire and I went about rounding up the money from an investment group to pay for it.

Les asked me and our corporate spokesperson, Skip King, to produce some names for what we would call the resort. Skip and I went to the Sunday River Brewpub one night and after a couple of beers produced what we thought would be a winner. We liked The Canyons. We brought it to Les the next day, and he liked it and said, "It's done. Get the naming rights to The Canyons." I have always been proud to tell people that I helped name it.

By this point, American Ski Company, which was formerly called LBO Holdings, was being recognized by Wall Street as a growth company and would need more capital. Big business has a built-in progressive system that passes your company from the debt bankers to the equity bankers, who could raise huge money by taking you public. Our Bear Stearns bankers were there to help us.

I am proud to say that The Canyons was eventually bought by Vail Resorts and then merged with Park City Mountain Resort and is now part of the largest ski resort in North America. I love sitting on a chairlift with strangers and telling them about my involvement in its purchase and growth. It is truly my home resort. I guess it was not a dump after all.

As American Ski Company continued to grow in 1996 and 1997, we would find ourselves in a position of needing to raise additional capital for the purchase of the two properties owned by Komori, a Japanese company. We were thrilled to have a chance to buy Steamboat Ski Resort in Colorado and Heavenly Ski Resort in California. Both were very high-end ski resorts with great reputations.

We had just completed our offer to purchase Wolf Mountain in Park City, Utah from Kenny Griswold and Michael Baker. That purchase was being funded by a loan of $60 million from Cerberus Capital. I was the lead person in the negotiations with Steamboat and Heavenly and was working with a representative from Komori Corporation out of Japan. This was quite an experience for me. First off, the time zone difference was about 13 hours, which always made it difficult to communicate with him. Second, the obvious differences in our cultures and language created a barrier. I remember calling him one morning and he was completely drunk. What a call that turned out to be. I got a lot of concessions due to his state of mind.

I recall one big final negotiation meeting with them at our law office in New York City when we were trying to close the deal. It happened to be July 30th which is my birthday. I was desperately hoping to be able to get up that evening to Poughkeepsie to celebrate my birthday with my sister and her husband, Mike, and my parents, who I had not seen in a while.

As usual, Les, Chris Howard, and I were dressed in casual summer clothes. I was wearing boat shoes with no socks—after all, who wears socks with boat shoes in the summer? During an exceptionally long day at the negotiating table, I wound up slipping my shoes off and without giving it a lot of thought, I put my feet up on the conference room table, facing in the direction of each of the Japanese management team from Komori. They never said anything, and I did not give a thought to it being an issue. The meeting finally ended, and the bankers provided a car to drive me to Poughkeepsie, which was about an hour and a half away. I arrived late for dinner, but I was happy to be there with my parents. In the conversation over dinner my sister asked me what the meeting was like and noticed that I was not wearing socks. She casually asked, "Tell me you didn't show them your bare feet."

I looked at her strangely and said, "What?" She repeated, "You didn't take your shoes off in front of the Japanese team, did you?" Suddenly, it hit me that I had and nodded yes. She then said, "It is an extremely rude gesture for you to show your feet to any Japanese people." I am thinking, "Oh crap. If this deal blows apart cause of that, I am toast." I qualified for having insulted them unknowingly, but that is a poor excuse.

Luckily, we resumed negotiating the next morning and the deal was finally finalized, but again, with some drama. I had been negotiating with them for a couple of months and we had conceptually agreed to a price of $280 million. As we sat in the conference room negotiating terms, we kept noticing that one of the management team reps was getting faxes and was reading them and then sharing them right in front of us. I could not help wondering if they were mad at me for the bare feet thing. We had a suspicion that our chief competitor to purchase the resorts, which was Booth Creek Holdings owned by George Gillett, was still bidding on them. Our curiosity was finally piqued, and we confronted them and found out that indeed, as we were negotiating a closing price, these faxes were for the latest offers coming in from the Gillette group. We were appalled, but there was not a deal signed as of that point, so there was nothing we could do other than put our best foot forward, no pun intended. We wound up with a final purchase price of $288 million and the papers were signed. It was by far the largest deal we had done to date and one of the largest in ski resort history.

As busy as our acquisitions had made us, Les had placed me in charge of getting the Sunday River Golf Course started, which included negotiating a construction contract with Trent Jones Jr., a nationally famous golf course architect. He was a very smart guy, and I was impressed with his style and demeanor. I was proud to negotiate and sign a contract with him, which he admitted was much lower than his normal pricing, but he really wanted to build this course in the mountains of Maine because he did not have any courses there.

Trent and his team spent months studying and then drawing the site plans. He called me one day and said he was ready to make a presentation to us. Trent sent the plans to me in advance so I could review them and show Les the drawings. As always, Les had his thoughts after I showed them to him. He had one idea that he thought was very innovative.

On the day of the meeting, Les and I met with Trent and one of his team members and I made the introductions in the conference room. In their respective sports, golf and skiing, both were industry leaders and well respected. It was cool to be able to finally have them meet and shake hands, not knowing what would result.

Trent started off with some pleasantries, but quickly got into explaining the drawings. Les was anxious to present his novel idea and within minutes interrupted Trent and said, "I wanted to throw an idea out here. What I hate about playing golf is getting stuck behind slow players and not being able to play through them. So why not build a duplicate par three hole at the fourth hole? If a foursome wants to play through, they ring a bell and play the duplicate hole to pass the foursome in front."

I was laughing inside thinking this response ought to be interesting. Well, Trent looked at Les and said, "Les, that is an interesting idea. In fact, my father tried that idea on a course in Chicago he built years ago, but it failed miserably. Now, let us get back to your drawings."

I had never seen Les put down like that before. The golf guy knew more than the ski guy about the golf business. The course did finally get built and it is truly a place of beauty, and I am proud to say I had something to do with it.

Our resort acquisitions were setting us up to have to take the company public. Our need for capital to pay for Steamboat and Heavenly could not come from debt, as we were already overleveraged, so we had to sell equity in our expanding company. This scared Les. He was used to being in charge and did not like the idea of having a board to report to and more importantly, not having 100% ownership. With no other options, we began the process to take ASC public immediately. We hired as our primary securities firm Donaldson, Lufkin & Jenrette with help from Furman Selz, Morgan Stanley, Dean Witter, and Schroeder & Company Inc. These were all reputable Wall Street companies and, since we were just a bunch of ski company guys, we needed not only their help, but their guidance.

We hired a financial consultant to assist us who had become close friends with Les. His name was Paul Wachter. He was an independent banker who specialized in hospitality resort companies like ours. He lived in New York, he was Jewish, he loved to ski, and our story, so we all hit it off well. Chris Howard, who was now on our staff as our chief counsel, would play an integral part in us going public. His legal background was just what we needed, and he could understand the big picture of what needed to happen and put the puzzle pieces together.

The process of going public is quite interesting. Ultimately, it comes down to trying to determine the correct valuation of the company. All factors are considered, including EBITDA (earnings before interest, taxes, depreciation, and amortization), assets, liabilities, and the net worth of the company.

One thing that was noticeably clear was that Les wanted to maintain at least a 51% ownership to still have voting control. Fifty-one percent was not going to occur unless he went on the market and bought a bunch of shares himself. This became an interesting challenge as he needed to produce some $20 million to do so. He certainly did not have that laying around in cash, so the next best thing was his very lucrative family-owned paintings by artists Van Gogh and Rembrandt that were in his mother's house in Teaneck, N.J. He was able to obtain a margin loan for the $20 million using the paintings as collateral. It would later turn out to be a big mistake when the stock price plummeted.

The Wall Street firms we hired all had a specific portion of the book to sell. They would go to their clients, tell them about the company, and then give them a rough approximation of what the stock price will be. It was not that easy a sale as we would be heavily in debt and dependent on growing EBITDA and real estate sales.

Les, Chris, and I were all part of the "roadshow," which is where the executive management team and the bankers all begin to visit different cities in the U.S. and Europe. The goal was to promote the company and stock and its growth potential so that stock could be sold. In a day, we would fly to three or four different cities, make our sales pitch, and then fly to the next city and do it over again. Fortunately for us, at that point we had leased a corporate jet that we were able to use, even though it was expensive, but our time was precious, and it was more convenient. We did not have to go through the public air terminals, as we would go to the private aviation companies to board our plane. It was a grueling schedule that lasted for the better part of a month. Lots of chicken dinners and presentations to investment groups. We did a tour of most major U.S. cities, including New York, Boston, Pittsburg, Minneapolis, Atlanta, San Francisco, and Los Angeles. The highlight was when we flew over to Europe in the Concorde supersonic jet. Meetings were scheduled for us in London, Paris, Brussels, Zurich, Amsterdam, and Geneva.

Amsterdam was quite an experience. Our bankers from Donaldson, Lufkin & Jennrette (DLJ) took us to a private club. In order to get in you had to be approved at the door through a sliding window. We did not know what to expect and I was surprised to see that you could get marijuana at the bar. It was Amsterdam, so there were plenty of beautiful women in scantily dressed clothes that were there to entertain us. Pot was openly on the bar, and I remember sneaking a hit so Les would not see me smoking. We partied there for quite a while before we went down to the Red-Light District where hookers position themselves in windows, so men could look and then select one. I declined a selection.

It was quite the evening and one I will never forget. I woke up with the worst hangover ever and so did Les, who was not a big drinker. We were complete basket cases as we got into the limo to take us to Holland for another roadshow appearance. After we fell asleep in the backseat with our heads resting against one another, the bankers took one look at our sad situation and told the limo driver to take us back to the private airport. We took off for London and a return trip back to the States on the Concorde. It had been a whirlwind excursion and a hard to forget experience in my life. After all, not everyone gets to take a company public.

Prior to the actual day of going public, I spent many, many hours and days with our lawyers, bankers, and auditors in conference rooms in a high rise in New York City, writing, rewriting, editing, and rewriting the prospectus. It needed to tell our complete company story and needed to be completely accurate. I depended on two of my key guys, Chris Lavek and Dan Kashman, who were back in Maine at corporate headquarters, to continually feed me the information we needed. They were consolidating all the financials of our current resorts and the three ski resorts we were buying, all of which had to be reviewed and audited by Price Waterhouse. The lead partner out of Boston for Price Waterhouse was a jovial, Irish guy named Jack McKinnon. He was a big Boston College and Notre Dame college sports fan. We got along great.

Wall Street bankers and corporate auditors were accustomed to doing this kind of tedious work. They had lower-level financial analysts available to them 20 hours a day. After we would finally go to bed, which was never early, those guys would continue to work into the wee hours. It was a grueling pace with constant demands, stress, long hours, switching of gears, eating poorly, and the list just goes on and on. But it did not take me long, based on my financial estimates, to realize what it would be worth to me on a personal level with all the shares I was going to be granted. There was an end game insight, and I knew it. For years, Les had controlled the company in its entirety, and I was now going to get "my share" for having helped grow it as big as it had become.

The big day finally arrived on November 6th, 1997. This was important, and my excitement level was high. With the help and support of many ASC staff members we even managed to bring a couple of truckloads of manufactured snow down to Wall Street, and built a ski run right out in front of the Stock Exchange on Wall Street. Before the market opened, Les, Chris, and I attended a breakfast in the New York Stockbrokers Club and became official lifetime members. We were treated like royalty, as we were that day's Stock Exchange featured IPO company. We were interviewed on TV by various financial networks and there was a lot of hope and optimism as the stock finally settled in at $18 per share. We had sold 14,750,000 shares of common stock on the NASDAQ Stock Exchange under the symbol SKI and had raised $265,500,000. I was going to receive grants of stock options for 100,334 shares of stock with an unexercised value of up to $2.8 million dollars.

My annual compensation that year was $170,000 and would now grow to $230,000. I recall my father reading the prospectus, seeing my salary, and commenting, "You made more money last year then I made in my entire career." That was a striking comment. I had become the senior vice president, chief financial officer, and treasurer as well as a board member on the board of directors of a publicly traded company. I knew he was especially proud of me. It was hard to believe for a guy that some 14 years earlier had been a paid firefighter in Poughkeepsie, N.Y.

After an initial surge that got the stock as high as $21 per share, we fell back by the end of a fast-paced day. Unfortunately, I had to go downtown with Chris Howard right before the closing bell to deal with some problems with the rating agency, so I was not on the podium with Les when he closed out the day by ringing the bell on the stock exchange. I was a little disappointed but considering how much money I had theoretically just earned; I could easily let it slide.

Les had come a long way in the ski industry and was now the King of the Mountain, but it did not always look that he would be. His father was a wealthy German Jewish industrialist at the start of World War II. At some point, he was arrested by the Nazis under Hitler's direction, but his lawyer was able to get him out on bond. While in Germany, he had, over the years, built up an amazing collection of original Rembrandts and Van Gogh oil paintings. As he prepared to flee to Austria, he did not want to leave them behind, so he cut them out of the frames, rolled them up, and took them with him as he and his wife fled and escaped imprisonment and/or death. At some point, they immigrated to Teaneck, New Jersey. For years, unbeknownst to others, that tiny home held some of the world's most priceless paintings by two of the world's most famous artists. It was a little unassuming Cape Cod house.

Les was born and raised in that small home in Teaneck. After graduating from Ithaca College, he started his career at Killington Ski Resort in the management trainee program. After showing some real potential, he was asked to go to Maine to Sunday River Ski Resort as assistant general manager. Ultimately, in 1980 he wound up buying it from Ski Ltd. and at the age of 30, he owned and operated a ski resort in Maine. His father never really liked the fact that he was in the ski industry. He thought that it was a waste of his time and felt he would never make anything of it or himself. Les loved his father dearly, but he did not accept any of his recommendations. He saw something that only driving entrepreneurs have a vision for and he would begin a journey that took him to Wall Street on this day.

We finished an exhausting day and flew back to Bethel in our privately-owned twin-engine turbo prop plane. Me, Les, and the pilot, Dan Bilodeau, landed at the Bethel Airport on a quarter moon night. I will never forget what happened then. Upon our landing and to my surprise, Les got off the plane and looked up into the moonlit sky and the eternal heavens and yelled, "Dad, look at me now! I am worth 350 million dollars!!!!" Tears came to both our eyes, and we hugged it out. His dreams had come true, and I had helped him get there.

His words spoke volumes. In speaking to his dad that night, I think Les wanted to tell him that indeed he had made it and that his father could be immensely proud of his son at that moment. It was a moment that I will never forget. It was not only touching for him, but for me as well, as it was the culmination of many years of challenging work, and I knew that I and others in the company had helped make this happen for him. We were all driven to grow the company, sometimes blindly, yet with a passion most companies did not have, which made up for our blindness. His favorite saying about staff was, "He/she just doesn't get it," or "He/she gets it." If you "got it" you were likely to stay for the ride. Obviously, I got it and what a ride it was.

I was appreciative to have been a part of this amazing experience. In my wildest dreams I would never have imagined that when I left the fire service 14 years earlier, my life and career would turn out like it did. I was enormously proud of myself, as was Teri.

I was at the pinnacle of my work life and yet, I still questioned if I would go back to wearing women's clothes in private. It was driving me crazy that the hectic pace I was maintaining prohibited me from doing so. I had to put this desire aside until things settled down, from a work perspective.

In my time as CFO for American Ski Company I would help raise over $900 million in equity and/or debt for the company. However, I was riding a wave that would soon come crashing down.

Teri and I went out to an American Ski Company Quarterly Board meeting in Lake Tahoe, the home of our recently acquired Heavenly Ski Resort, in the summer of 1998. Our stock price had dropped from the initial IPO price of $18 to around $12, a drop that was of concern to our stock analysts and shareholders. Analysts were feeling the pressure to lower expectations as we were coming off a severe weather year and missed hitting our numbers. In a private meeting of certain board members, it was discussed moving me out of the CFO position to a resort position and bring in someone with more public company CFO experience. I could agree with the logic. In a series of senior management changes, I was moved to Managing Director/President of Sugarbush Resort in Vermont. I had an amazing ride for five years and although disappointed that I was leaving as CFO, I was going to a resort that I thought I could find independence and happiness in running.

Off to Sugarbush Teri and I went. We bought a fixer upper house with an unfinished garage/loft foundation on upper Stagecoach Road in Fayston, Vermont with amazing views of both Sugarbush South (Mt. Ellen) and Mad River Glen Ski Resort, a neighboring old school resort owned by a co-op group of diehard Mad River skiers. I met my senior management staff and could see that me coming in after the popular managing director, Rich McGarry, was transferred was not going to be easy. It turns out that they were not big fans of Les Otten nor ASC, all of which I represented. I could always sense that I was being talked about and not in an effective way and in some cases being sabotaged.

At the start of my second ski season, we opened early with a three-foot storm in mid- November, which enabled us to open two weeks before Thanksgiving. There is an old saying in Vermont that goes, "Wait five minutes and the weather changes." Over the next two weeks it rained and got warm, and we had to close as the holiday weekend approached. I got a phone call from Les yelling at me for not figuring out how to stay open. He was being irrational, so I hung up on him. He called me back and fired me, saying that the managers there did not like me. It was that quick. I even had a panic attack, which scared those in the office, when I came running out of my office screaming in pain.

When I had a chance to reflect in the days that followed, I felt a true sense of relief. I accepted a termination package, so I would leave peacefully and financially stable. I immediately cashed in my options, which I could now do, before the stock retreated any further. I cashed out at about $12/share and walked away with over $1.8 million before taxes, which came out to $900,000. Almost all the other senior managers, who had options like I had waited too long and most got nothing, like Les, who lost all $350 million he had theoretically made when we went public.

I had started in June 1993 with Les and ended our relationship in November 1999. It was an amazing six years and I achieved more than I could have ever imagined. I was not sure what would happen next, but I wanted to change things up. Teri and I talked about our options.

I was not looking long and came across an opportunity to consult on a proposed new ski resort to be built in Tamarack, Idaho. The developer/owner was a rich French guy. I was asked to review the financials and comment on the proforma they had developed. I worked with some talented ski and finance business folks in that deal. I thought they were reaching for the moon in their projections and tried to tell them that, but they were hell bent on making it work. Once my consulting project was done, I let them go on their way. The resort struggled to make a go of it and eventually went bankrupt a few years later.

I was fortunate to have some great experiences while serving as Managing Director/President of Sugarbush Resort.

In the fall of 1999, the marketing director, Dave Dillon, got a call from the Vermont Republican party stating that George W. Bush would be making a campaign stop in Vermont and they wondered if Sugarbush Resort would be interested in hosting a dinner/ fundraising rally. He asked what I thought, and I gave a resounding yes. I thought it sounded like a great idea. We formed a committee to lay out the plans. It would be held in our fitness center on the tennis courts, which would require some modifications, but was very doable. It would be a very high-end dinner with state and local dignitaries on hand and lots of wealthy Republican donors. Security was intense and Secret Service agents made their presence felt. My staff did a phenomenal job organizing and delivering an amazing dinner. When the big day arrived, I had the opportunity to greet the future President when he pulled up in his caravan to be escorted into the hall. He was a friendly guy, smaller than I thought he would be, and gave a resounding campaign speech that was well received. The event came off flawlessly and the staff was rightfully proud of what we pulled off. It was to be his only stop in Vermont. I cannot say I voted for him, but I have great memories of the evening and of having met a president.

In the winter of 1998-99, which was my first as the head of Sugarbush, Mad River Glen Ski Resort was having a celebration of their 50th year in business. I was invited to attend as President of Sugarbush, as Mad River Glenn was a neighboring ski resort. Over the years, there was not a lot of love between the two competing resorts as many felt Mad River was a skier's mountain that catered to locals and, in fact, had sold shares of the resort to over 1800 dedicated skiers when the original owners decided to sell. What made it such a unique place was the single chair that was built in 1948 and to this day is the main chairlift to the top, although it was replaced with a similar single chair in 2007. It has a long, proud history with a slogan that has garnered world-wide attention. It reads, "Mad River Glen: Ski it if you can!" It is rightfully deserved as it is an exceedingly difficult, steep, limited snowmaking resort. On the other hand, Sugarbush was known as Mascara Mountain, as it catered to the wealthy from big eastern cities and was the complete dichotomy to Mad River. Over the years the two resorts were never friendly towards one another, despite being in the same community. I saw an opportunity to try to change this perception and came upon a large color photo of the two resorts from an overhead plane. It was beautiful winter picture on a bluebird day with the trails covered in snow. It looked like one large ski resort and my goal was to try to unite the feelings of the two resorts, so the community felt we were one large ski family. I presented it to the general manager and my short emotional talk was well received and, for the moment, bonded us as never before.

Sugarbush has an airport for smaller planes but is more recognized for its hang-gliding operations. I often saw them gliding around in the sky and thought how cool it must be, but always had a fear that something could go wrong. When the opportunity came up to take a complimentary glider flight, I thought twice about it, but decided I wanted to try it. On a beautiful summer day in 1999 I drove to the airport with great trepidation. I was warmly greeted by the pilot who offered me some words of encouragement and we boarded the glider. It is unique to be going airborne in a plane with no engine, tethered to a gas-powered plane. The takeoff was exceptionally smooth and when we reached about three thousand feet in elevation the tether was released and off we glided. It was glorious and my fears were momentarily erased. We circled around, only being kept up by the wind. It was euphoric and one of the best 15 minutes I have ever experienced. The views of Sugarbush Valley were spectacular. I was in a headset and was told that we would be beginning our approach to land. Then the fear crept in again. But the pilot was skillful and landed with ease. We came to a halt and got out of the plane. Although I did not kiss the ground, I certainly appreciated it more and walked away with a special appreciation for gliding.

One day in August 1999, I got a call from Charlie Sullivan, a good friend whom I had worked with at Sunday River. I had played a lot of golf with him over the years and loved his company. He was a good Irishman, who loved stories, laughing, and his cocktails, so we got along well.

He said to me, "How would you like to play in an amateur Ryder Cup tournament against players from England? It is going to be held at three different courses over three days. The first day at Ocean Edge, a course on Cape Cod, then Cranwell Resort in Lennox, and lastly at the Worcester Country Club, all in Massachusetts. This is the same course that the Ryder Cup was first played in 1927."

I responded with a resounding, "Absolutely! Sign me up."

He then asked, "Do you know of anyone else who is a good golfer that would want to play? The U.S. needs another player."

I then said, "Let me check with my friend Brian Ganey." Charlie also knew him. "He's a good golfer and likes to have fun." I called him right away. "Brian, do you want to play in the amateur version of the Ryder Cup between our United States team and a team from Great Britain?

Brian responded with, "Is this a joke?"

Well, in fairness to him, it did sound fishy. Out of the clear blue I asked him if he wants to play in the amateur version of the Ryder Cup between a United States team and a team from Great Britain? If you are a golfer the Ryder Cup is like the Holy Grail of the sport, only possibly bettered by the Masters. To think we would be playing in the amateur version was too crazy to believe.

I said, "No, this is for real."

I told him the details. "In that case, I'm in!" said Brian.

I was psyched. Two of my best friends on a road trip to play in a golf tournament of this significance. We later learned that the team from England had to play in qualifiers to become eligible. We were a bunch of nobodies who said, "Yeah, I'll play" when no one else would.

The tournament was played in early September. The three of us met up and drove down to Cape Cod together where the first match was to be played. The matches would be played in the same format as the original Ryder Cup, which had Foursome matches (alternate shot), Four Ball (best ball of team) and Individual match play (pitting players against their opponents by hole).

We all met in the Ocean Edge Country Club event hall for a social the night before the matches and to meet the other team. What a great bunch of players from England they turned out to be. Like us, they had players of varying ability and handicaps. They liked to drink (a lot), laugh, and tell golf stories, so they were just like us. Both teams had a woman player and the person representing the U.S. team was an attractive, 40ish woman from Pittsfield, Mass. named Norma Probst. Charlie and I were both married, but Brian was not and was looking for his soulmate, so Charlie and I immediately had the mandatory discussion with Brian, which went something like, "You better hit on her and soon or someone else will!"

We all chatted together and hit it off. It turned out that Norma was the Marketing Director for Cranwell Golf Resort in Lennox, Massachusetts. She was attractive, athletic, outgoing, and fun to be with. Brian was smitten. Over the course of the three days, we all would spend a lot of fun times together. They truly bonded together, and their relationship exists to this day.

I do not recall my results from the two days of team matches, but I vividly remember the individual matches on the day at Worcester Country Club. It was forecasted to rain and, sure enough, the prediction was accurate. It poured the entire day. My opponent was a decent player, but he was not playing well in the rain. I was winning handily when he made the decision to forfeit the rest of the match on the 13th hole. I had won, although it was not really a test of golf, but survival of the fittest.

We assembled in the country club bar and waited for the others to finish. We were sipping cocktails and having hors d'oeuvres. Most of the men's matches were being forfeited because of the rain or were over, but Norma was still out there battling with her opponent in the pouring rain. As they climbed up the hill on the 18th hole, the match was tied. It was amazing to watch them walking up the fairway in the heavy, cool rain, holding umbrellas, with a caddie in tow.

We yelled loudly, "USA, USA, USA!" trying to cheer Norma on. She hit her second shot on the par four short of the green and had a long chip shot facing her. Her opponent was on the green in two and would be putting. Norma was up first and hit a decent chip but left herself with a long par putt. Her opponent putted first and left a short putt for par. Norma needed to make her putt or the match would go to her opponent. We all were rooting for our respective teammates, and it had a sense of drama that would be hard to play out again, especially with it raining as hard as it was. It was the perfect climax to an exciting week of golf. Brian went up to her on the green and gave her a big, heartfelt hug. He had just lost his match on the 18th hole after facing elimination on the 15th, so he knew her pain. The irony of a bunch of men standing out on a veranda in the rain watching two women battle it out was not lost on me or the others. I was in awe of Norma's tenacity and grit and so was Brian. Her putt did not go in and Norma lost, but she certainly gained some big fans in Brian, Charlie, me, and the rest of our team.

Unfortunately, we lost to the Brits soundly. Following the match, we were welcomed into the main dining hall for a ceremony in true Ryder Cup custom, including bagpipe music, both teams walking into their national anthem, and finally, an inspirational talk to us by Bob Cousy, the former

Celtics basketball star. It was night that I will never forget and left me grateful for the opportunity to have played in this tournament.

That night, we stayed at the Holiday Inn in Worcester, Massachusetts after playing another round at Worcester Country Club. We went for another drink in the bar that night and after a while I said my goodnights and headed off to bed and left Brian hanging with Norma at the bar. Their relationship was off and running. Around 3 a.m. that night, the fire alarm went off in the hotel and we were told on the loudspeaker to evacuate. There was no fire and it turned out that Northeastern was playing Holy Cross in a football game the next day and someone from Holy Cross had pulled the fire box to disrupt the Northeastern player's sleep. Pretty clever, but disruptive for the rest of us staying there.

I am happy to say that Brian and Norma have been together ever since that tournament. They live in Pittsfield, Massachusetts in a beautiful home and have enjoyed working and living in this ski and golf resort community. They have remained Teri and my best friends over the years. We love to spend time with each other.

Once again, I found myself fortunate to have done something that most amateur golfers would never get a chance to do, which was to play for and represent your country. I only had a small dose of what the real Ryder Cup must be like, but it was incredible, and I would soon experience the real thing as a golf fan.

The same month after my return from the amateur Ryder Cup, I was offered an opportunity to attend the actual 33rd Ryder Cup in Brookline, Massachusetts as I was given free tickets to the entire tournament by Budweiser, a sponsor at Sugarbush. I was thrilled. Teri gave me the okay to go and I jumped on it as the chance to attend the "Battle of Brookline" was a once in a lifetime opportunity.

Little did I know that us fans would be witnessing one of the most significant sporting events of all time. The first couple days of play left the U.S. team behind by a score of 10 to 6. No team had ever come back from that big of a deficit playing the individual matches, but Team Captain Ben Crenshaw believed in his players and left them inspired in the team meeting with an unforgettable quote, "I'm a big believer in fate!"

On that Sunday, after a couple of days of uninspired play by the U.S. team, I called Teri that morning before the matches and told her, "I will likely be leaving early if things didn't start to look better for the U.S. team."

Sunday at the Ryder Cup is always an exciting day, and the course was overflowing with patriotic fans. The sun was shining, and optimism abounded, despite the large deficit. Chants of "USA, USA, USA" could be heard in the distance. If the U.S. team could come back to win, it would be historical.

I planted myself early that sunny Sunday morning high in the grandstands on the 15th hole where I could get a view of not only the 15th fairway and green, but the tee shot and green on the 16th and all the play on the 17th, which was behind the grandstand I was sitting on. The day started well for the U.S. team, and they built leads in most of the early matches. Us fans could buy and listen to the play on a radio headset and watch play on an overhead video monitor, so we were able to keep on top of what was going on.

The excitement level grew all day long and became electric. The U.S. won the first five matches and took the lead quickly. The team was also ahead in a couple of the other matches, and it looked like they could pull it off and win. I remember Tiger Woods coming up the 15th fairway with a huge crowd of fans following. He was still relatively young, and his career was just taking off, but he was already the real star of the team. He easily won his match.

"USA, USA, USA!" was all you could hear throughout the grounds. The excitement reached a crescendo as Justin Leonard putted on the 17th hole. The putt would guarantee a tie and would virtually clinch the Cup for the U.S. I was standing on the top of the grandstands watching the play come up the 17th. When Leonard made that 45-foot-long putt to secure at least a tie, pure bedlam ensued.

The behavior of the U.S. team and fans was criticized after they raucously invaded the 17th green after Leonard had sunk his long putt, but before Jose Olazabal had attempted his shorter putt.

I hugged an elderly woman next to me, who was screaming, "We won, we won, we won," but Olazabal still had to miss his putt, which he finally did after the lengthy American celebration. It was thrilling and matched the same feeling I had when the U.S.A. beat the Soviet Union in the 1980 Olympic hockey game, which I also attended. I am quite sure that there are not too many people on this planet that can say that they attended BOTH spectacular sporting events, which have long been at the top of the greatest sporting events ever.

As I think back on these amazing experiences, they once again demonstrate the intrinsic value of sports, including the significance of friendship, camaraderie, patriotism, and healthy team or individual athletic competition. That month of Ryder Cup experiences was a once in a lifetime opportunity and I am truly thankful to have been in the right position at the right time to have been able to do both.

A "Mudder" in Hartford

In June of 1999 while working at Sugarbush as Managing Director, I got offered the opportunity to play the Hartford Open course immediately after the PGA tournament had been played, so it was in tournament condition with long, thick roughs and lightning-fast greens. Anytime you can play a PGA tournament course is an honor. It was an amateur outing with about forty players in total.

I remember getting a speeding ticket on the way down from Vermont to meet my best man and friend Brian Ganey as we were playing together. The day was not starting off well.

The weather was horrible, and we began to play in pouring rain and it did not let up all day. We were playing in a stroke-play tournament, which means all your strokes count. If you have a bad hole, you must post that score. I have always been a good "mudder," which is another way of saying I play well in the rain, and this day was no exception. I made some amazing shots and wound up shooting a smooth 74, about four strokes below my handicap. I never felt any pressure, and everything just happened naturally despite the terrible conditions.

It was one of the highlights of my golfing career. I recall the party after where I was announced as the winner. The pro said, "How in the world did you manage to shoot a 74 in today's weather on this course? Simply incredible. I do not think some of the pros from this past weekend's tournament could have done that today." Some days are better than others and this was one of those days that I played well above my true abilities. It is what makes golf great. Every day is different as it is you against the course and your score tells the tale.

Teri and I were spending the winter of 1999-2000 at Sugarbush, but my termination made us rethink everything. We had recently renovated the house and enjoyed its newness, so we were not in a great hurry, especially since I had cashed out and pocketed some decent money.

In early 2000, we talked about our options and we both seemed interested in owning and operating a bed and breakfast. We looked at one in Woodstock, Vermont, but settled on a fifteen room B&B on Martha's Vineyard called the Hanover House and we closed on April 30, 2000. We were so excited. I can remember Teri, while walking home from a closing dinner celebration on Main Street in Tisbury with our family, pulling me into a store alcove hugging me and saying ecstatically, "I can't believe we are living on Martha's Vineyard and own our own B&B." She was as happy as I have ever seen her. We ran it together and grew the business over the next three years. One moment I will never forget is when Teri and I watched the events of 9/11 in the office of the inn. We hugged and cried together in complete amazement that this had happened to our country.

Lots of wonderful things happened while there, including smoking pot with my daughter Lindsay for the first time. She had come down to the Vineyard on the day of the closing to help us celebrate. We were all out back on a large deck drinking, laughing, and having fun. Out of the clear blue, someone lit up a joint and started passing it around. It came to me, and I took a hit. Lindsay was standing next to me, so without even thinking I passed it on to her. She took a hit and then realized what had just happened. She started laughing and called her sister Erin to tell her what had happened. It would not be the last time I embarrassed her.

In 2003, we wound up selling Hanover House to the innkeeper next door. He was also a bidder when we bought it originally and bought it from us for $1,000,000 more than what he was first bidding three years prior. It was a great sale for us.

After selling the inn, we had lots of cash and needed to reinvest it, so we found a nursery/garden center in West Tisbury that the owners were selling after 20 years. We had no clue as to how to run a garden nursery, but that did not stop us. We hired a young couple, who were getting married, as general managers, which included them living in a nice Cape Cod house on the property. They both had some agriculture background and were offered an Option and Right of First Refusal to buy the property in eight years. We all learned quickly, and our first season came off very well, despite some long-time Vineyarders thinking Teri and I could not pull it off. I would do the bookkeeping and marketing while Teri helped with management and production. Mike and Kerry were the perfect partners and worked their tails off. The nursery was highly respected on the island, and we were proud to be the owners.

Owning the nursery gave us the opportunity to bring home plants to our newly constructed home. After a couple of years our terraced garden was strikingly beautiful and loaded with blue hydrangeas. We owned the nursey until 2008 when we decided to sell it early to our general managers as we were moving to Utah. They accepted the deal, but had it financed by the Small Business Administration. One of their requirements was that we take back a second mortgage note for 20% of the sales price and effectively all our profit. I was not happy about it, but as it turns out, this requirement was a lifesaver. Once the recession hit in late 2008, we wound up living off that monthly payment for years and they never missed a payment.

In 2000, a good friend at the time, Joe Eldridge, bought an 800-acre ranch in Kamas, Utah. He wanted to create a dude ranch for tourists. Teri and I were hired to be the hospitality managers of the ranch. Not only did we get paid, but we lived in a guest house on the property for free. It was a fun job with little stress. We skied a ton, rode horses in summer and winter, went snowmobiling, and hosted great parties. We loved spending the winters in Utah, and we fell in love with the Kamas area. In 2004, the ranch boss approached Teri and me about buying his newly built home as he could not afford it. In exchange, they could move into the guest house and live free. We jumped at the chance for only $209,000 and still live in this house, which has truly become our forever home.

Teri and I owned three beautiful homes/properties at one time, starting in 2004. We decided to start renting them out when we were not staying in them. I also rented my friend's ranch and got a commission for doing so. It kept me busy as I discovered the key was to respond quickly to inquiries, which I was particularly good at doing. We made some good money renting out our homes over the years. They were all beautiful and located in desirable places: Martha's Vineyard, Sarasota, Florida, and near Park City, Utah.

In 2005, I had an idea to put together a group of friends to form an investment syndicate. We would collectively evaluate real estate and business opportunities and decide if it was a business or property that we wanted to invest in. We did a couple of projects with one being a condominium contract flip at Jiminy Peak, thanks to Brian Ganey, which was very profitable. This same group also invested 20% with me and Teri as the 80% majority owners of a Beadniks (bead) franchise of a local Martha's Vineyard bead store and its owners Craig and Sally, who were our close friends.

At one point in the mid-2000s, Teri and I had so many things going it was insane. We owned the garden/nursery, Heather Gardens, I was the managing partner of the Fairwinds Development building 12 affordable homes, we developed and opened the bead franchise in Sarasota, Florida in St. Armand's Circle, we were renovating and flipping houses in Florida at University Park Country Club, I was renting out our homes while not in them, I was building modular homes on the Vineyard, including our own new home, and yet we still managed most weekends to have house guests.

I managed our business and household finances, which was quite a task. As I look back on this time, I once again was peaking in my business skills, except now it was for our own profit, not someone else. I will not lie, it was challenging. Money was going out fast and it seemed like it never came in fast enough. I did the books and the tax returns for all these businesses, which was mind blowing during tax season. I was juggling bank lines of credit, credit cards, vendors, politics, and personalities and yet, at the end of the day (that now-famous Wall Street saying), we were successful.

Thank God for the invention of cell phones as I was able to run all these businesses from wherever we were. My friends started to call me "'Telephone Tommy" as I was always on the phone. I loved the independence of being an entrepreneur. I was always busy. I can look back at this entrepreneurial timeframe with immense pride. We were living an incredible lifestyle, but in 2007 it was becoming clear to me that something had to give.

The Big Scams

Over the years I have met some interesting and impactful people, but none so much as a woman named Bari Emmons turned out to be. It was 2002 and Teri and I had been on Martha's Vineyard for two years and were proud owners of our bed and breakfast, The Hanover House. We always had some guests that would reach out and be a little friendlier than others. Bari was just one of those people. She checked in late one night and paid by check.

She was a smaller, heavy, older woman, in her sixties. She always looked disheveled, and chain smoked. We pegged her as someone eccentric, yet we did not question her. We never gave a thought that she might be a person who might not be who she says she is.

I was surprised when within a few days her check bounced. Back then, that was not unusual on Martha's Vineyard, so I did not think much of it, especially when she told me she would cover it as she waited for a large wire transfer to come in.

She wound up staying a few days and told us a story about how her mother was very wealthy and had recently died and left her a fortune that she would be inheriting and getting shortly. She wanted to settle on Martha's Vineyard, which, coincidentally, has been recognized as a place that people have migrated to hide from their past. She fit that bill perfectly, in retrospect. She listened intently as I told her about my CFO background and asked, "Would you be interested in being my business manager? I need help with all this money. I will pay you a healthy salary." It was too good to believe, and I quickly and naively accepted the offer.

She needed a place to stay while looking and then buying a home on the Vineyard, so we suggested our guest cottage, which we normally rented out daily. It was a beautiful cottage that we had renovated from a storage building into a warm, inviting two-room guest house. It was very cozy and overlooked our beautiful gardens and a courtyard. It rented for $350 per night, but I was willing to let her pay us when the inheritance transfer came in.

Another concern was that with her living on our property, I would not be able to dress as Cami as frequently as I was. Many days, after Teri had gone to the B&B for work, I would dress up only to clean up before she got home. I suffered through it knowing that it was worth it.

As for managing her financial investments, I asked my advisor, Ken McEwan, from Salomon Smith Barney to get involved. He and I discussed a strategy and he suggested bringing in a team of advisors. They wanted to meet with her, so all these high-powered financial advisors flew into the Vineyard from New York City one night for a dinner party that Teri and I would host. It was a beautiful summer evening with a full moon. Our dinner space was in an old glass greenhouse that had been converted into our living and dining area. At night, and with proper lighting, the place looked magical.

Bari was on her game and told them her story and we discussed how to best invest her money. We were all pinching ourselves as $90 million was a lot of money even in the world of Wall Street. We produced a game plan and waited for the money to be delivered.

I asked my business partner in the Fairwinds project, Ed, who was a local realtor, to help her in searching for homes, and expensive ones at that, so he jumped at it. We found a quintessential Vineyard home on the water in Vineyard Haven. It was a 6,000 square foot Cape Cod with gardens, decks, a gourmet kitchen, and a boat dock and launch. She signed a purchase and sale agreement and paid the down payment via a check.

One day she even said, "Why don't you and Teri also look for a new home? I will buy it for you as kind of a bonus for helping me out and getting settled." We were excited and could not believe our good fortune. We found the perfect waterfront home nearby to where her new home would be. As her business manager, it made sense to be close to her and who would not want a home right on the water?

Her story needed to start to come to fruition as far as receiving the money so ultimately, she told us that her banker from NYC was flying into the Vineyard. It was a foggy day and Ed and I drove out to the airport to pick him up. We learned he was not on the plane.

On the same day, the check she wrote for the down payments on the houses bounced. We were all getting suspicious and challenged her, but again she produced a story that we fell for. This delay had gone on for a month. One would have thought, being the intelligent person, I was supposed to be, that something was amiss. We were seeking the pot of gold at the end of the rainbow and were oblivious to what was really happening, which was that we were being conned and scammed.

I kept pressuring her and finally started feeling that something was terribly wrong. She eventually came clean with me. I reported her to the police and sure enough, back came a mug shot from a previous time she tried to pull off the same fraud on the mainland. We had been hoodwinked. Luckily, Teri and I really did not lose much of our money, $9,000 in lost rental revenue, but we never saw any of hers after honestly thinking we would. I was humbled and embarrassed as I had friends and others who got involved like lawyers, real estate agents, financial advisors, and appraisers who did lose money. It would cost me some of these relationships as they had lost their trust in me.

We eventually got over it and moved on. Unfortunately, another year or so later, I met John, a tree vendor for Heather Gardens, our garden/ nursery, through the course of normal business. John told me about an investment group where he had invested some of his and his brother's money. It sounded like a worthwhile investment opportunity and a sure thing. I jumped in with both feet and invested $25K. When it came time for payback, it was delayed. I smelled a problem. I had gotten the name of the actual investor in the Midwest. I communicated with him directly to get answers and he provided me with a bunch of backup material that gave me some comfort. I even invested another $15K based on his word that it was happening soon.

You are thinking what a jerk I was, and you are right. Sure enough, I got defrauded again. I reported it to the police, and they did go after him, but I never got any money back. John, the vendor who turned me onto him, also supposedly lost his investment. In thinking about it, I eventually began to think that he was a partner in this fraud, but I never chased that angle. He was very Christian, Lutheran I believe, and seemed like a good person, so I never questioned him. I never tied anything directly to him other then he gave me the investors name, but I often wonder.

How could anyone get involved in two frauds in such a brief period? Well, I did, and I could not believe it either. I cannot really blame Teri as she always had reservations about both and warned me. How did I let this happen and what was the lesson I would learn?

Trust should be earned not just given out freely. I am and always will be a trusting person. I just find it hard to believe that people would intentionally defraud or try to financially harm another. It is not in my DNA to think differently. In both cases, I was too trusting and greedy. I should have had my radar up, especially after the first time. I was very gullible and fraud artists know how to recognize that easily and then exploit it. False trust, greed, and being gullible all combined can only lead to problems. Maybe being conned is a guy thing, as I am sure Cami would never have fallen for them.

Over last 40 years I have had a love affair with businesses and real estate. In fact, many family members and friends would say I was "addicted to the deal." I had hits and I had misses. I like to remember the good ones, but it is hard to forget the bad ones. My partner in these deals was Teri, although occasionally I wondered off track and did deals with friends that I sometimes came to regret as something would inevitably go wrong. I did lose some friendships because of it, and I came to realize that uncomfortable feeling when you're mad at a friend or they are mad at you. Unfortunately for me, when I get mad, I confront the person about it very quickly. In any case, I have done many real estate deals in my lifetime, and I have opened my fair share of businesses.

Many of these real estate deals in Florida and on Martha's Vineyard were in the 2000s. We wound up buying our first Sarasota home in University Park in 2003. We found a small fixer upper with a cute courtyard and hot tub as well as a separate guest house. It needed cosmetic work, which both Teri and I enjoyed doing and coordinating. In a brief time, we had improved its appearance significantly and although our original thought was not to flip the house, we recognized that it was a seller's market and that we could make a quick $50K. s We found another house that needed upgrading and sold the first one and rolled the profit into the second. We did a facelift, such as painting, flooring, and cabinets. The value grew quickly as the market for homes in Florida was red hot.

Our intention was to keep this second home as it was on the golf course in a nice community. A neighboring home went on the market, so we bought that one as well with intentions to fix it up, which we began. It did not take long in the crazy real estate market that had developed for us to find another home that was improved but did not need any work. We cashed in on the other two, selling one to friends from Martha's Vineyard. We rolled all the profits into the newest house and like climbing a step ladder, we wound up with a gorgeous home, but as it turns out, a very hefty mortgage payment. We loved the University Park community, and I became active in the HOA. We were active golfers and enjoyed the country club and its amenities, especially the Friday night socials.

We were living the good life. We were the youngest couple as I was around fifty and Teri was mid-forties. We got along great with our new friends and loved the Sarasota scene. We often ate at nice restaurants with our friends and went dancing at clubs. We belonged to the Country Club and became typical active members. We are both beach people, so many days we would be at Siesta Key or Lido Key beaches. We felt we had quasi-retired, although I always remained busy with my businesses and Teri still worked at Heather Gardens during the summer months while we lived on the Vineyard. It was a good life as we also had bought a home in the Park City area and would rotate between all three.

In the summer of 2001, a friend, Ed Herzeg, who lived on the Vineyard and was a fellow bed and breakfast owner, approached me about joining in on a development project in the Town of Tisbury that he and another one of his friends, Jim Stevenson, were beginning. It intrigued me for several reasons. It had enormous potential for income with not that much risk or cash outlay. If built, it would benefit those individuals that needed "affordable" housing, which covered the good feeling aspect. It also was remarkably close to a lot that I had purchased and would be building a home on, so it would not be a burden to get to. I was not so sure about the partners and what role we would take on. Since my specialty is finance, I was asked to handle the financial affairs. Ed was a realtor and oversaw sales and Jim handled getting permits and other logistics. He had done the original work to "find" the opportunity.

The project involved a 12-acre parcel of land that had been deemed "undevelopable" due to zoning issues years prior. The homeowners around this land always felt it would be green space in perpetuity; however, in the state of Massachusetts, there was an affordable housing statute called "40B", which in effect, allowed these "undevelopable" parcels of land to be developed if certain affordable housing criteria were met. We knew it might present issues and could wind up being a protracted process, but we borrowed some bank money and with our sweat equity, we pressed on. We hired a reputable attorney on the Vineyard, Marcia Cini. She had done some real estate closing work for me and Ed in the past and she had a good relationship with the local zoning board in Tisbury.

We approached the first meeting with apprehension, but we were very prepared. We had even gone to Canada to check out modular home companies as that was how we would build the homes. I was driving and approached the border crossing. The border agent asked, "Why are you guys coming into Canada?" I said, "We are checking out modular home companies here as we are building an affordable housing project on Martha's Vineyard." He looked at us and said, "Affordable homes on Martha's Vineyard, now that's an oxymoron."

The local paper had authored a bias story about our application, so the locals were fired up. We had asked for thirty-two homes to be built on the twelve acres. It would be cluster housing, with a mix of single family and townhomes that covered the low, mid, and full price markets, which was required in the 40B application.

It was aggressive application, and we found out quickly that getting all thirty-two units approved would not only be difficult, but impossible. The Zoning Board ordered the application to go before the Martha's Vineyard Commission, which is an environmental approval board that handles special situations that might have an impact on the environment, traffic, and character of Martha's Vineyard. Going through them was going to be another arduous process, with lots of meetings, legal bills, studies, and headaches.

They would eventually study every aspect of our project, from house design to road construction to planting of trees to block visibility. It was some pain in the ass and would take a year and a half to complete.

As time dragged on, it became obvious to me and Ed that Jim was not going to be able to handle his responsibilities without our help, specifically mine. I became the de facto lead developer and did most of the presentations at these meetings. It was a good thing I did as the Commission and the Board had confidence in me leading this project and living up to the restrictions and requirements. I had allies on the Board that supported affordable housing on the Vineyard, which had been a hot topic for years with extraordinarily little to show for it. This development would be one of the first major affordable housing project on the Vineyard. At some point in this grueling process, the realities of making good money were overcome by the desire to get these homes approved for those who needed the housing. I was driven to get it approved and worked my butt off to do so. I had other business obligations going on, either the bed and breakfast or the garden/nursery, while working on getting approvals, so I was out straight for years. I loved every minute of it, despite the stress.

Once again to relieve the stress, I found myself increasingly dressing in secret. While Teri was out working, I would "work" from home, which included getting dressed up in her lingerie. I was always so embarrassed and fearful, but I enjoyed the feeling. Wearing stockings and a bra was a thrill. I needed it.

The process dragged on and on and rolled into a second year. This was a slow process that I did my best to speed along, but my hands were often tied while waiting on others and meetings to occur. After a grueling process, which included the project being shrunk down on our part to twenty-four, then sixteen, and finally fourteen units, we got approval from the Martha's Vineyard Commission. However, we still had to go back to the zoning board in Tisbury for approval. I did have an ally on the board, Jeff Kristal. He was fair and lived by the rules, which really made it hard for them not to approve the project as there was no legal reason not to. After over two years in the planning, we finally got approval in mid-2003 from the board, where we eventually negotiated it down to twelve units in ten structures.

One of the highlights of the project after approval was the night that applicants for the affordable homes came together for a lottery drawing to determine who would get the low- and mid-income homes. When the winners were announced, there was much excitement. I felt like I was truly helping those in need. I would work closely with these families in planning their new home. I did an excellent job for them, although in trying to protect the shrinking profits, I had to say no often to improvements they wanted.

The final project was to consist of four low-income houses, two mid-income houses and six full priced homes. The homes were not going to be stick built, but modular homes from Excel Homes in Pennsylvania. They would be trucked up in pieces to the barge site in New Bedford, Massachusetts, then would be barged over to Vineyard Haven into Packer's

Wharf. From there, I would have them transported to the building site with a police escort. Most would come as four boxes and would result in a Cape Cod-style home being assembled in one day. There was a finishing crew that I would hire to "button up" the house, which included final shingling and siding.

We had determined the economics would only work by doing modular homes and we were proven correct. We knew to the penny what our profit would be on each home. There was truly little variable in home costs due to the 40B restrictions and we had no problem finding applicants in all three categories. The full rate homes were still a great bargain by Vineyard standards and sold quickly. Our sales manager, Ed, did not have a lot of work to do on his end as they sold themselves and we had a list of potential buyers who had signed up.

We started construction in late 2003. I took the lead as far as construction being started and accomplished. I had hired a fellow volunteer firefighter with Tisbury Fire Department, Andy Dixon, as Project Manager, responsible for building the units, coordinating subs, and other responsibilities. He also committed to buying one of the units. He worked extremely hard over the next few years, and I am thankful to have had him managing the project. It was never easy, and it took a lot of my management and leadership skills to overcome each obstacle as they came up.

By 2007, the project was complete, and I am happy to say we all made a lot of money, but well within what the 40B regulations stipulated. The partnership was not without its issues, however.

One partner, Ed, who was a good friend at the start, was overpaid by $10,000, which was caused by a mistake by our attorney at the closing of the last home. I noticed it when reconciling the transaction and I told him about it. He had moved to Portland, Maine and had become a useless partner to me. He oversaw real estate sales, which anyone could have done as the sales all came to us before being built. I asked him to keep his third, but to pay me and the other partner our one-third shares. He refused, and it created a big problem, and I was furious. I have never been so mad at someone in my life. Our friendship ended in a screaming match, which did nothing for me except I once again learned to not do business deals with friends. Luckily, a homeowner to whom the business had extended a short-term loan, paid it off and we were able to recover our shares of the profit.

I wound up taking on most of the burden to get it done, from project approval to overseeing construction to dealing with the town to completing financial forms for the 40B and dealing with the community where I was well known. As I look back upon it, I can honestly say that it was the most significant challenge I was ever faced with and accomplished, which includes rescuing people in fires to taking American Ski Company public.

There were times when I was on Main Street in Vineyard Haven, and I could feel people looking at me with animosity. I respected their opinion, but at the end of the day, I know that what we built was needed and done well. The project was called Fairwinds, but clearly the name did not reflect the actual tornado that took place. I did learn that I could handle being scrutinized, hated, and talked about. It was good training for what it would take when I finally came out as trans in later years.

Beadniks

In 2005, Teri and I decided to open a Beadnik franchise, a high-end retail store that sells beads and jewelry. Our friends from Martha's Vineyard, Sally and Craig, had franchised their business, which Sally had successfully started on the Vineyard years prior. We would open the business on St. Armand's Circle, which was in the Lido Beach area of Sarasota. St. Armand's Circle was one of the most successful shopping areas in the world. We found a fantastic location next door to Columbia Restaurant, which had been the most popular restaurant for 80 years. We were excited to be their first franchise and set out to renovate the space. It was a big capital project at over $500,000, and I knew I needed more capital. I had started an investment group with some good friends, including Scott Karn, Brian Ganey, Joe Eldridge, and Steve Ellicott. This was to be our first combined project and they each put in $20,000. I put in over $400,000, so Teri and I had 80% majority ownership.

I asked my daughter Erin, who had been working on Wall Street after college, to be the general manager, and she accepted and moved to Sarasota. I was thrilled to think that I had provided an opportunity for my daughter to come work for me and that we would grow this business and that one day she would take over ownership. We completed the renovation and opened in early 2006. The store came out beautifully, thanks to the arduous work of everyone, including Sally and Craig.

Everyone was proud, and we had an opening party that was well attended by friends from afar and in Sarasota. At the end of the evening and after some party cocktails, I threw on a beautiful jade necklace. I pranced around, thrilled to have a piece of woman's jewelry on. Everyone laughed at me, but little did they know that I was doing it more often than one could imagine. Ironically, Teri agreed to work at the store part time when we were in Sarasota, so while she worked, I would be at our beautiful home often dressed in her apparel.

The first year of the store was great. The real estate market was still hot, people had discretionary income, and we did well—well enough to pay my daughter a healthy salary, but not enough for the partnership to make any money back on their investment. Each subsequent year got more difficult as the economy began to suffer. We wound up losing money every year and took our respective share of those losses, which helped some of us with our taxes.

I learned some valuable lessons. I had sold friends on the potential of profits and although they understood the risks, the outcome was not what I or they wanted. Luckily, we did have another real estate flip that earned us all back a healthy return, which offset some of the cash loss we all took and kept the troops at bay. Keep in mind, the partners collectively owned 20% and I owned 80%. When the business started to require an infusion of cash and losses were obvious, they stopped contributing and I did it alone, thereby increasing my share and decreasing theirs, but they did not care about that, they just did not want to put in any more cash into a sinking ship. Once again, doing business with friends is always risky and luckily, I never lost their friendships, but in looking back at it, it was not worth the chance.

Although my intentions with Erin were noble, she stayed three years in a business that was losing money and ended up moving back up to New England to seek other employment. I think she would agree that those three years were not the best of her life, but we managed to survive the experience.

Once again, I learned that if you are getting your family involved in a business, be aware of the risks both are taking. Also, do not bet on your friends having a magic bullet that will generate profits for you. I believed in their concept of a high-end bead store and saw visions of profits based on what turned out to be unrealistic proformas. It all added up to be another big mistake on my part. After three years and a big capital investment, we left St. Armand's and moved the business to Park City, where we were moving full time.

We opened in Park City just as the recession started in October 2008, and although the store was beautiful, discretionary income of our customers was sinking fast and after three years we closed in June 2011. I never calculated the final cash loss as I do not want to know, but it is safe to say that I lost $500,000 over those years. It wound up being a huge blow to us financially, which would significantly impact the next few years and how we lived.

In late-August 2004, Teri and I were at our Sarasota house when we heard about Hurricane Frances, which was expected to hit the west coast of Florida in Ft. Meyers and then head up toward Sarasota. It had winds up to 145 miles per hour, which was alarming. It roared through Cuba along the way and killed many and caused millions of dollars of damage. When hurricanes are likely to hit Florida, they become the topic of everyone's conversation and concern. It becomes an obsession the likes of which I had never seen. It reminded me of my last hurricane.

I had been through a hurricane in Poughkeepsie, N.Y. back in 1976. It was more like a tropical depression at that point after coming up the coast and it roared into town late one night. I had been a volunteer firefighter for a few years and had just gotten hired as a paid firefighter. A first alarm came in for wires down along Rt. 9. Engine 5 and Truck 2 were to respond. Drivers would be at the station quickly to drive the rigs to the scene, so I responded from home in my sleek 1974 Pontiac Grand Am to the scene.

It was my first sports car, and it was gorgeous. It had a lime-colored body with a split top with removeable glass on one half and white leather the other. It had a two-barrel, 250 horsepower V-8 engine, with a white leather interior. It was my pride and joy; it was flashy and fit my personality perfectly. I think the first sign of my female side coming out was in picking the color. Firehouse friends were making fun of me, but I couldn't care less. It was beautiful. I loved driving it around town.

The call was handled quickly on our end, and Central Hudson Power was called to the scene to clean things up. My brother John was also a firefighter and had driven Engine 5 to the call. We all headed back to the firehouse because we were being placed on standby, which meant we were to hang out waiting for calls, which were expected to pick up due to the storm. John left the scene a few minutes before me in the engine.

I was driving along Rt. 9 and remember the winds were howling. I would look up at the streetlamps and catch a glimpse of the torrents of rain being whipped by the wind. It was like a movie scene. Out of nowhere, a huge maple tree along the side of the road came crashing down onto the highway, landing right on top of the engine of the car. I came to an abrupt stop and was thrown around, as those were pre-seatbelt days. I was startled and had a slight cut on my head and was bruised, but no serious injuries. The roof of the car and the engine compartment hood were crushed. Windshield glass pieces were everywhere.

The fire station was staffed, and someone had called for help, so they responded quickly as the accident was within a mile of the firehouse. My brother drove Engine 5 to the scene and recognized my car immediately. In a panicked voice he screamed, "Are you okay?!" I responded, "I am fine, but the car looks totaled. The tree came out of nowhere and there was nothing I could do." I was heartbroken that my dream car was severely damaged, but thankful to be alive. I did get the car fixed, but it was never the same and I sold it within a year.

Remembering that hurricane experience, I realized the damage a storm could do, so Teri and I took all the precautions we could. This was the first time our Florida home would go through a storm with us there. We did not have hurricane windows, but wished we did. We brought what we could inside and left the patio furniture in the pool, so it would not fly around. The rain was heavy, and flooding began. It turns out that there was not a pool overflow drain, so the rainwater filled the pool quickly and started to creep up in the lanai area. We were two inches away from it coming in the house, but the rain subsided just in time and the water level receded. It was an intense experience. The noise made it sound like a locomotive was headed toward us. I quickly realized that hurricanes are nothing to fool with. We survived with minimal damage to one of the screens on the lanai and some debris to clean up. We got lucky and said, "See ya, Frances" thinking we would not see the storm again.

Two days later, we flew back to Martha's Vineyard to our other home. On the drive home, I heard Frances was coming up the east coast and headed right for the Vineyard after leaving Florida. I thought it was very unusual for someone to go through the same hurricane twice but figured it had happened before.

The storm had become a tropical depression and was headed up the east coast with winds in the 40 mile-per-hour range but was still expected to bring heavy rains that could produce flooding. Once again, I prepared for the worst. I was also a volunteer firefighter for Tisbury Fire Department on the island and thought back to the car accident in 1976. 'Better be careful,' I thought.

Our house had just been completed that summer and we had not faced a storm like this yet. We battened down the hatches and waited it out. We were becoming veterans of this storm. The storm was not as intense as it had been in Florida, but it was still scary. There was flooding in our back courtyard, but not enough to do any severe damage, except for minor flooding in the basement. We had dodged a bullet the second time in a week and once again we bid farewell to Frances, or so we thought.

My daughter Lindsay's wedding was coming up the next weekend. It was a beautiful affair in a Boston suburb at a golf country club. It turns out one of my closest friend's daughters was getting married in Ireland after that same weekend. We took a red eye from Boston the night after the wedding and headed to Ireland, where neither Teri nor I had been for a vacation.

We landed in Shannon and headed down the west coast. The scenery was breathtaking, and we had mild weather the first few days. We hooked up with some friends who also came over for the wedding. The wedding itself was beautiful, and the ceremony overlooked the ocean and took place in a small, ancient chapel.

I played some great golf courses while there including Lahinch,

started by the legendary Tom Morris in 1894. It is famous for one hole that has a huge hill in the middle of the fairway where a ranger stands up top and waves a red or green flag to let you know when it is okay to hit your second shot to protect the golfers on the other side of the hill. We also played Doonbeg, a new Greg Norman designed course. Both were beautiful with grand views of the water. I had hoped to play Bally Bunion, which is a fixture in the top one hundred golf courses in the world, but we were on a tight schedule and all we had time for was to do a drive by and check it out one day.

We knew our luck would run out with the weather and, as it turned out, we had not seen the last of Hurricane Frances. It took a week, but it had churned its way across the Atlantic Ocean after hitting the Vineyard and was headed directly toward Ireland.

It did not seem possible, but sure enough the day we were passing through Bally Bunion, it hit land again. The winds were fierce, especially since it was a seaside course. We arrived to find to our amazement that there were golfers playing despite the hurricane. The had paid their $250 in advance to play this historic course and nothing was going to stop them. Teri and I sat in our rental car watching with amazement and laughing as these crazy men (a woman would never have been so stupid) played the course. They do not allow electric carts, so you must use a pull cart. The carts were being swept away in the wind. The flagstick was bending over halfway. How they could play even one hole was amazing. It was a crazy scene and one I will never forget.

We continued to the Ring of Kerry, which is a 111-mile drive around the Iveraugh Peninsula. The views are of a rugged and verdant coastal landscape and rural seaside villages. It would have been spectacular, but the rain was heavy with fierce winds. Between driving on the wrong side of the roads, which are narrow to begin with, and the poor visibility, it was downright scary. When we finally admitted to each other, "I'm scared," we realized we still had seventy-five miles to go to complete the drive as it was one way only. When we finally finished with our nerves shattered, it did not take long for us to drive to the nearest pub for a well-deserved drink. Frances had impacted us again, some 4,028 miles from where we met it the first time.

As crazy as it sounds, in a span of two weeks we managed to find ourselves in the same hurricane three times in three wildly different places. We headed back home and bid a final fond farewell to a crazy weather event named Frances.

I have researched this on the internet, and no one ever has reported accomplishing this feat. Teri and I might be the only people in the world to have done this.

Over the years, Teri and I have spent many weeks at timeshares we purchased in Mexico. As crazy as it sounds, we have owned three different timeshares from three different timeshare companies. We bought one in the 1990s while visiting the Dominican Republic. The resort company is called Viva, and over the years we have enjoyed their Mexican properties in Playa Del Carmen. We also bought from Palace Resorts with more beautiful resorts in Cancun, Cozumel, and Playa Del Carmen, including an adult only resort, where we thoroughly enjoy vacationing. Finally, we purchased weeks from Palace Resorts with properties in similar areas. The other two were supposed to be absorbed by Palace Resorts in the deal, but they never pursued the closing documents, so we wound up with all three. That also means that I have not been able to say NO to timeshare sales pitches three times. In fact, there was even a fourth timeshare that we got sucked into. It was in Playa Del Carmen and was on the Playa Del Carmen golf course. It was beautiful and luxurious. We visited twice in a brief time span one fall, but decided to cancel the deal, which we could still do. We felt that some "promises" made would not be fulfilled. Unfortunately, they did not want to cancel the deal as promised, so I ended up charging them back on the credit card, which began an exhaustive and frustrating experience, which I finally prevailed in winning.

We are now left with hundreds of vacation weeks available to us, of which, even in a good year, we might use two weeks. The good news is that none have a yearly maintenance fee attached. We simply pay for a week when we want to go.

On one of those trips, we took a day trip over to Cozumel to check out the island. Cozumel is known for a few things. It is a destination port for cruise ships. It has beautiful coral reefs, and the scuba diving and snorkeling is recognized as some of the best in the world. It is also known for its jewelry shops in the main part of town. With thousands of tourists coming off the boats daily, these shops push though lots of business to unsuspecting tourists, like me. Teri and I were celebrating our 10th wedding anniversary and I wanted to get her a new, bigger diamond. She loved the idea and so we found ourselves in a diamond shop being romanced by your typical pushy jewelry salesperson. He took us to lunch as the diamond was being appraised. The appraisal came back with extremely high marks for clarity, cut, color, and carat weight. We were sold and for $10,000 we left with a beautiful new diamond for Teri. Ironically, I looked at the beauty of this ring and thought to myself how nice that would look on me as well.

When we got home, we notified the insurance company and they requested that an American appraisal company needed to reappraise the ring for insurance purposes. Thinking nothing of it we took it down to our favorite jewelry store in Vineyard Haven called Moonstone. We knew the owner well and trusted her. She came back with some astonishing results. The clarity and color were not what was originally reported through the Mexican appraisal. During this time, we were also fighting with the timeshare company for a refund, but I began the process to complain. After repeated, expensive calls to Mexico, we were getting nowhere with them, so again, I called the credit card company to charge the purchase back. I got conditional credit while they pursued them. We still had the ring in our possession, and they figured out we were not going away any time soon, so they reached out to us and suggested that we meet them in Playa Del Carmen at our Viva Resort property and switch the ring to a better cut and clarity model.

We went down to Mexico and met with them again. The new ring had been appraised by them on Cozumel and of course the result came back with higher color and clarity marks, so we made the switch. I am still not sure how they could not think that we would not have it appraised by our jeweler again, but we did and although she said it was a better ring, it still was not as advertised. I notified them that the chargeback would continue, and the credit card company supported us. The company sent the jeweler a note and we waited to see what they wanted to do. We were in the driver's seat as we had the ring and the $10,000 credit. We waited and waited and waited and to our surprise, they never pursued us to return the ring.

Teri still wears the ring to this day and although it was not what we hoped for and expected, a free diamond ring made the experience worth it. At the end of the day, I cannot tell you how frustrated we both were and how many countless hours I spent on the phone or dealing with this. It was worth more than $10,000, so I do not feel bad that we kept the ring.

I learned lots of lessons from this experience. Unfortunately, when travelling abroad, Americans and our money become targets for ruthless companies. This showed me that nothing is life is ever free without working for it.

While owning the B&B and living in some cramped owners' quarters, we found an amazing home in Vineyard Haven to purchase. It was a renovated New Hampshire home built in the late 1700s that had been disassembled and moved to the Vineyard. It had seven-foot low ceilings with lots of post and beam, a beautiful greenhouse that was converted into a family room, a gorgeous courtyard with gardens, and a large garage that we quickly converted into an adorable guest house that we rented out through our B&B. It was in town and close to the B&B. It was our dream home, or so we thought.

In 2004, a couple building lots became available just up from Lake Tashmoo that we looked at and thought had lots of potential, so we bought both. Teri and I decided to build a home on one of the lots thinking we would flip it. It was assembled from eleven modular units that would be put together resulting in a beautiful 4,500 square foot home. We loved Lake Tashmoo and had direct access to it via a deeded easement to the lake. When the house was completed, we fell in love with it and decided to sell our in-town home (at a good profit) and live in the new one. It became our new dream home with a beautiful kitchen where Teri loved to entertain. We had an amazing back courtyard with gorgeous gardens. The second lot we sold to a local Vineyard couple, Leslie Graham and Capt. Teddy Karolekis for $500k, making a nice profit. They built a beautiful home and becoming our close friends.

In early summer 2008, Teri and I sat on our porch of the Vineyard house, looking down at the lake, sipping our nightly cocktails and had a major discussion about our future and where we would live. We weighed keeping the Vineyard house, but it did not make sense as the mortgage was huge and although we loved the summers there, we did not like being stuck on the island during the winters. Sarasota was a viable option, but again the mortgage was huge, and we did not think we could live in Florida in the heat of the summer. I told her, "We can't keep making these huge mortgage payments, especially on the Vineyard and Florida house." I looked at refinancing and was told by the bank that we were not in default and there was nothing they could do for us, implying to stop making payments, so we decided to do just that on those two homes and see what develops.

The houses went on the market in 2009 along with many other homes from people like us who were overleveraged. Although they were both beautiful homes, they sat there unsold for 18 months. We kept lowering the price, but still nothing. Finally, the bank, which was Countrywide, who later would go bankrupt, started foreclosure proceedings on both and put them up for short sales. We were renting them whenever we could and did still go to them, but only for short vacations. We held our last big Vineyard blowout party in October 2009 for Teri's 50th birthday and it was a fond farewell. All our close friends and family came, and it was a night to remember, although bittersweet. We loved that Vineyard home, having built it ourselves and took immense pride in it. It had beautiful gardens loaded with blue hydrangeas thanks to our ownership in our nursery/garden center.

These decisions left us with our best and only living option, which was our home near Park City. We loved the summers there and being skiers, the winters were more than welcomed.

We had bought the house in 2004 from the ranch boss at the Diamond J Ranch. Teri and I were running the ranch as the hospitality managers in the winters when the B&B was quiet for a friend who owned it. The ranch boss had built the home, but could not afford the mortgage, so he asked us if we would buy it so that he could move into the ranch's guest house where we were staying for free. We loved the area, so (and in hindsight, thank God) we bought it from him. At the time I thought, "What is one more house?" It was brand new and was the perfect ski getaway. It is a blessing we bought it.

Money was tight, but we were surviving as we had sold the garden center in 2008 to the general manager, which was a pre-arranged deal when he was hired. We ended up taking back a second mortgage on the business as he did an SBA loan, and the bank would not loan him the money unless we held a sizable second. I can recall being angry that we did not get all our money at closing as it was to be our profit. As it turns out, thank God we had that income stream going forward as he was diligent about paying on time and it kept us going at a time when we needed income.

It was not until May of 2010 that the Vineyard and Sarasota homes sold under short sales at crazy low prices within a week of each other. Once closed, we were driving into Park City to celebrate on a beautiful spring evening with the top down in our shiny red Audi convertible. Teri has always trusted me with our finances and was aware of what was going on but did not know all the dirty details. She asked, "So how did this turn out financially for us?" She knew we were losing money; she just did not know how much. I responded, "How much do you think we lost?" She said, "I don't know, $250k?" I laughed and said, "Not even close. Try $750k." She looked at me in disbelief and said, "And we're going out celebrating?" I said, "Well, the bleeding is over, and we can finally move on." It was utterly amazing that we survived all of this as we really had gotten ourselves (and I take the blame as I was "addicted to the deal") in a financial mess.

Teri was always a rock and willing to do whatever it took to make these businesses work. She was totally involved in running the B&B, helped manage the garden center becoming quite knowledgeable on plants and how to grow them, and then ran the retail bead store.

In 2011, after we closed Beadniks, Teri wanted to find work and applied for an $11/hour job as a front desk person at the health clinic in Park City. She did not get hired! We were shocked and amazed, but about a month later she got a call to ask if she was still interested and since she had not found anything yet, she took the job. As I author this book in 2022, I am proud to say she was the RN Clinical Manager at the new Intermountain

Urgent Care/Work Med Clinic, managing the entire operation for over seven years. She is simply amazing in so many ways. I could not have found a better business and life-long partner.

It was a crazy 11-year stretch of entrepreneurialism. As I look back on it and write about it, it sounds worse than it was living through it.

In 2008, we made the decision to move full time to Utah and sell our Vineyard and Sarasota homes. Teri and I still owned Beadniks, located in Sarasota, Florida in the tourist shopping area known as St. Armands Circle, but the lease was ending. When we left the Vineyard, we moved the store to Park City. Teri would become the full-time manager and I would handle marketing, accounting, and work it part-time. Unfortunately, we finished the Park City store in September 2008, just before the recession started in October. It did not take us long to figure out our timing was not good. We were a discretionary spending business for the most part and we immediately saw a drop in business after being open for a while. It was a beautiful store with lots of colorful wall hangings, bead tables, and copper paint that gave the store an authentic, Tibetan feel.

Teri managed the store's day-to-day operations and was good at handling clients and sales. She blossomed. I remember one Halloween I dressed up as Cami in a seductive miniskirt, beautiful wig, and makeup to give out candy. The neighboring shopkeeper saw me and was amazed at how good I looked. She said, "This doesn't look like the first time you've dressed up, you're too good at it" with a smirk on her face. She had clocked me and years later when I came out, she said she knew it that day I had dressed in front of her. Oh well!

Our lease was coming due in 2011 and when I told the property owner we would not be re-signing, he offered us the opportunity to leave a few months early as he had someone else that wanted the space. We jumped at the chance and made the decision to close. Unfortunately, I had friends who had invested in the business and owned 20% between them. We were losing money year after year and other than the write-off they could take on their income tax return, it turned out to be a bad investment for all of us. In total, Teri and I lost over $500,000 with our only benefit coming from the tax write-off. It was a valuable lesson learned.

Once we made the decision to move out to Park City full time in the fall of 2008 and move Beadniks there, I started looking for some full-time work and applied and was hired as the Managing Director of Lespri Property Management, which was a boutique hotel and five-star restaurant as well as a large property management business, which oversaw rentals, housekeeping, and property management. The hotel and food operations were easy to manage, but the property management part was a disaster. They had poor record keeping, which left many owners complaining about revenues being low. I was constantly fielding complaint phone calls, which did not make the job fun. I was not happy with the job. I remember wearing women's lingerie often under my male attire to relieve the stress. I was still hiding this secret from my wife Teri but was getting closer to coming out to her.

While owning Beadniks, it made perfect sense to buy an earring display business where I would place a display in a spa or salon and the earrings would sell for $9.95 each. The owner would get 30% and I would get the rest. I had to go around and replenish used stock. It was mindless but spun off some cash, but I knew I needed to do more.

One day, I saw a want ad that struck my interest. A local non-profit agency was looking for an executive director for Summit County Beef, whose purpose was to raise and sell organic and hormone-free, grass-fed local beef to support local ranchers. It was a growing entity that Summit County started to foster the "support your local community" movement. I was hired and reported to a board of directors. My mission was simple: sell more product and make the community more aware. I was successful in my efforts, and it reached a point where the county wanted to sell the business to a for-profit entity through a bidding process. I was the perfect candidate to buy it and submitted a legitimate, winning bid. I would now own the business and was free to do as I wanted with it.

I did not do anything different in running the non-profit and made some easy money selling local beef. I was a frequent face around town as I went to farmers markets, the Park Silly Sunday Market, and other local fairs to sell.

In 2010, I met a guy named Glenn Cogan, who had started a local business called the Park City Local Card. Originally, he wanted me to become part of the program with Beadniks. Clients bought advertising emails that were sent to locals who had signed up for the card. They would be able to show the card, like a credit card, to a vendor and get a discount or whatever the offer was in the email. I thought it was a cool business model and when a chance to take it over became a possibility, I jumped on it. I had over 5,000 email addresses of locals. I would sell them advertising and then send out twice a week emails to the list with offers from the merchants. It was widely used. I operated this business until late 2014. At one point I expanded to the Sugarhouse area in Salt Lake City and started a local card program there for a merchant's association with whom I contracted.

I had been operating the beef company for a couple of years when I was approached by a local guy who wanted to buy some beef and proposition me about opening a butcher shop in Park City featuring Summit County Beef and other local and/or organic meats. The concept was intriguing. He had a friend who was a butcher who wanted to join the partnership. We formed a company called Park City Meat Company and opened in November 2013 after renovating a space in the Park Plaza. It was beautiful and looked like a classic old butcher shop. We opened to much fanfare and our first two months over the holidays were fantastic. After a few months, we were barely making ends meet and faced the realities that we were a specialty shop with higher prices then local grocery stores. Why would locals go out of their way to come to buy meat that is more expensive than the grocery stores, even if it was hormone free? Unfortunately, we thought of this after the fact. When business started to slow down through the summer I met with the partners and told them the realities that we had to close or keep throwing in more money, which neither partner wanted to do, but I was insisting something had to happen. We closed one year after opening. It was a great concept, just bad timing.

In July 2014, I got a phone call from a good friend, Bill Handler, who was a member of the Jewish Temple in Park City called Temple Har Shalom. He told me that the Temple was looking for a consultant to come in and clean up the books and assume temporary management as the executive director was being let go. It was to be a three-month position while they looked for a replacement. There was plenty to do and learn and I quickly became someone they could see as continuing in the position, so I was offered it full-time. I filled some staff positions and wound up with a talented team. Within a year, the place was humming along. I reported to a board of directors with extraordinarily strong type A personalities who at times were difficult to manage. Although I am not Jewish, I fit in well with the congregants and made many good friends. I had been raised a Catholic and was not practicing any religion, per se. In working there, I found religion again and enjoyed the spiritual side of working for a Temple. I retired in 2016 from the position. I was extremely fortunate in that I came out as transgender in late 2016, thanks to an accepting board and congregants. I am forever grateful to Temple Har Shalom. Working for them made an enormous difference in my life.

For over 15 years I have been going on a ski vacation to Killington Ski Resort in Vermont with some of my family and good friends on the same days in early February. In 2009, it started with myself, Scott Karn, Brian Ganey, and my brother Jim going up to Killington for a day trip. Conditions were great that day and we had an amazing ski day.

We stopped at Cooper's Cabin off the Glades chair, which has long been a place for summer and winter hikers to spend the night while walking the Appalachian and Long Trails. It is also a popular cabin for skiers, who can navigate the way down to it as it is a little moguly and narrow, to take a break and smoke some pot.

When he walked into the cabin in one of the early years, my brother Jim found some roaches on the wooden picnic table from a previous hiker and/or skier's hospitality. Not knowing the custom, which is that the former owner of the joint left it to <u>share</u> with subsequent visitors, Jim thought they were for the taking and stuck a couple in his pocket for his consumption. After Brian straightened him out, we enjoyed the remnants.

The next year rolled around, and the trip was opened to all after I suggested wives be invited. We decided to do a longer stay and rent a house in Pittsford for two nights and two days skiing. After 10 years we stopped for a couple years but picked it back up in 2022.

Over the years there had been some consistent attendees, including myself (and for two years Teri), Brian and his long-time partner Norma, Scott, Jim and his wife Holly, Steve Ellicott (and sometimes his wife Martha), my sister Terry and her husband Mike, and for the most recent few years some sailing girl friends of Scott, Mary Beth and her husband Mark, and cousin Brenda. Most of us share a few common traits, including that we are fanatic about skiing, we like having an enjoyable time, which includes dancing, eating tasty food, playing games, drinking, other adult things like "the green thing", and our lifelong friendships.

It is not for the faint of heart as most are New Yorkers with type A personalities, mixed with the proper amount of sarcasm and braggadocio. I have always been the "unofficial" timekeeper, the person who every ski morning must remind people that in 10 minutes we leave for the mountain and despite getting yelled at constantly, I serve my purpose. Although most of us know Killington well, I often am the skier they follow as I know my way around having worked there for 10 years. It is an especially important function, and I do not take it lightly, nor would they ever let me. I particularly like taking them up the "Ganjala" or in common ski terms the gondola, which we used for a different purpose, smoking pot.

The excitement that we all had that first day, which had always been a Wednesday, is a true rush. I have skied all over the U.S. over the years, but few resorts get me excited any longer. Snowbird and Alta usually do, but the Big K has always. When I come around the corner on Killington Road, where the mountain becomes visible, my stomach churns and the adrenaline begin to flow. The reason for me is simple: the mountain has some incredibly challenging terrain and it being an eastern resort with narrow trails with large crowds, one must be on their game. The conditions are often icy or scratchy, so when you're done skiing Killington for the day you can walk away proudly. I have had some amazing powder days over some 50 years that I have skied Killington, but most days were just groomed out runs where you could really ski fast.

We are all good skiers with some being a little better than others, which results in there usually being two groups after we all do a couple warm up runs together. We have had great luck over the years with minimal injuries. Steve has the record for worst fall. We were going down a trail called Panic Button on Needle's Eye Mountain one year. I took the lead and got a safe way down and then pulled over to wait for the others. Steve followed me down and just as I stopped, I saw him go flying off the side of the trail into some safety netting in the trees. I feared the worst as it looked ugly, but he climbed up the side back onto the trail and said he was fine. One lucky guy.

We have had some interesting weather over the years; typically, it is very cold, with some powder days sprinkled in to keep us always hoping the next trip will be the big year with the huge snow dump. 2016 stands out as the weirdest year of all. We knew the forecast called for warming temperatures and rain, and sure enough, we woke up Wednesday morning to pouring rain. Scott sat looking at the rain in the large picture window and kept saying, "It will get better." But it did not, so we went up to the Killington base lodge where we were welcomed by a wonderful guest service person named Chad. He told us the mountain was closed and that if it opened it would not be particularly good skiing. It did not take us long to determine we would not ski as the snow was turning to ice. Chad offered us a free voucher good for one year. When we realized that the temperatures were going to plummet overnight, we asked for a voucher for both days and he graciously did so. We were all so bummed and looked for a way to keep busy. I suggested bowling, so we called the lanes in Rutland, and they said come on down, so off we all went. It turned out to be a real blast. We turned disappointment into a day we will never forget.

We started our first dance party in 2010. It usually starts after some serious drinking and debauchery. We all love to dance and love music, but none more so than Steve. It is hard to even describe his passion other than visually. He comes to the trip with his own sound system and digital devices and sets up shop. The best part is that he also serves as the unofficial DJ. He loves it and we love him doing it as well, except when his love for reggae music precludes us from getting to hear what we would like. Volume is always a point of contention, proving you cannot please everyone, especially Norma. Steve liked to bring ham for a food choice. We all know that we are not getting fresh ham, but some left over from his Super Bowl party. His frugality is truly inspiring.

It is so much fun to see everyone's dancing moves, especially Scott, who has some remarkably interesting moves, likely because of his duck feet. His feet are wide, like a double E. It is hard to describe his dance style other then there is a lot of stomping and fast clapping of his hands. Incredibly unique and sadly funny.

You can tell when Brian is having fun when his face gets very red. But then again, his face is always very red. He is a smooth dancer, like his skiing, and likes to groove to his own beat. When he and Norma dance, it is a thing of beauty.

My brother Jim is an interesting dancer. Like his skiing, he is gangly, exciting, and unpredictable. It is usually best to stay out of his way and let him just do his thing because if one of his elbows hit you it could really hurt. The combination of Brian, Jim, and I make for an interesting trio while on the dance floor.

My sister Terry is very reserved when it comes to public displays, which is hard to believe being that she is a Richardson. What is surprising is that her husband, Mike, who is very shy and quiet, will occasionally dance up a storm. Makes me wonder if he is not a closet dancer and she keeps him secret.

The dance party ends at a reasonable hour as most of us have a good buzz and are jazzed to get to bed and be ready for skiing the next day.

Our dinners are usually hardy and ample. I typically make a meatball and sausage pasta sauce that we have with spaghetti and/or macaroni on the first night. I pride myself on my sauce and do spend a lot of time, money, and energy to get it prepared. During the first years, I would cook it at one of my daughters' and ruined many a good pot of theirs by burning the bottoms. Because of that, I started preparing it at home, freezing it and then bringing it with me. Teri thinks I am crazy, but I do it out of love for all these great people that I am lucky enough to call family or friends.

We have stayed at a few unusual places over the years, but for many years we settled into a place called the Tuck It Inn Chalet, which is on the Killington access road just above the Pickle Barrel. It is your classic ski chalet with lots of bedrooms a large dining/sitting area, hot tub, and easy access to the mountain. The first couple of years we stayed there, but we despised the bed situation, specifically the mattresses. After writing the owner and telling him that if he did not do something about it, we would leave, he made no move to improve the situation, so we did just that. Two years later, I received a note from him saying that he had taken our advice and the mattresses were replaced, so back we went to the Chalet after a two-year hiatus.

We typically end our day at the Killington Base Lodge bar, which has been an instrumental place in my life. When I was at Killington working as the controller/ Killington Base Lodge manager, I met my wife Teri there.

I cannot say that it has been easy for me to come back east each year. Some think I am crazy as why would I leave the skiing in Park City for that of Vermont, but some years it has been better skiing. I could never be accused of not wanting to have an enjoyable time, but a ski trip is never easy. When I transitioned, I needed to bring a lot more stuff. I worry about being seen not in girl mode and I am always trying to look my best.

I would not trade this trip for any other. I look forward to it each year and I enjoy the planning that goes into it. In fact, I just got back from our yearly trip, here in 2022.

In 2009, we were living out in the Park City area. Years earlier we had bought a building lot and had joined a private golf club called Tuhaye. We had bought this lot to eventually build our dream house, which never would come to be, as the recession hit us hard.

I played a lot of golf with another friend named Steve Elrich, who, like me, was able to play many days in the morning. We would go out early and finish eighteen holes in 2.5 hours. We were playing one Thursday morning when Steve began on a par three with a large vertical drop to the green. His ball landed, rolled up to the pin, and came within a fraction of a hair of going in. One third of the ball was over the hole, but it never dropped. He took his birdie, and we went on to the next hole. We both were wishing for just one more rotation of the ball, so he could have gotten his first hole-in-one.

The following Thursday we were out playing again, and we got to that same hole. Steve went up to tee off and I jokingly said to him, "Put a little bit more umph into it and maybe you'll get your hole-in-one." I then turned to get my golf club out of my bag and said to myself, "Or maybe I'll hit the hole in one." I realize we have all said that knowing it never happens.

I stepped up to the tee and hit the shot, which I would not call pretty by any means, as it was mishit. It landed on the green, but on a line drive. The green had just been aerated and the ball quickly rolled through the sandy, punched green and into the cup. I had hit a hole-in-one. I was ecstatic, and Steve was equally excited for me as well. We finished the round by 11:30 and went into the clubhouse. This was in the initial stages of the development's growth and there were not many golf members, especially not at 11:30 in the morning. I asked who I could buy drinks for, and the golf pro said, "Well since we can't drink and there's no one else here, you can buy Steve a drink but that's about it." It was even too early for Steve to drink, so I walked out of the clubhouse with the joy of knowing I hit a hole-in-one and never had to buy anyone a drink.

A Quick Joke

There was a time that I could tell jokes with the best of them. I had a whole repertoire of jokes but have forgotten most. My favorite and one that I have been telling since I was 18 years old is my "duck" joke. It goes as follows:

There once was this father who had three sons. One was smart, so he named him Smart. The second one was not as smart as the first one, so he named him Not So Smart. The last son was kinda dumb, so he named him Dumb. After several years, the father decided he wanted to test their intelligence. One day he called them all together and gave each one a duck and told them, "Go out and sell the duck and tonight we will see who did the best." Off they went.

Smart was so sure of himself that he simply walked down the road, stopped a woman approaching and asked, "How would you like to buy this duck?" She looked at it and said, "That's a good-looking duck you got there, I'll tell you what, I'll give you $2.50 for the duck." He quickly accepted the money and headed confidently home.

Not So Smart was walking down the road and was not sure how to sell the duck when out of the clear blue a man stopped him and said, "Nice looking duck. I'll give you $5 for the duck." He was surprised and took the money and headed home.

Dumb was walking down the street, scratching his head wondering how he would sell the duck. He stopped a beautiful woman walking down the street and asked, "Ma'am, how would you like to buy this duck?" She looked at it and wanted it. She said, "I would love that duck, but I have no money to pay for it. Tell you what, let us go to my apartment and I will let you fuck me for the duck." It did not take Dumb long to realize that was a good deal. Off they went to her place and consummated the deal. When they were done, she looked at him and said, "That was really good sex. Tell you what, I'll give you the duck back if you fuck me again." Dumb did not have to think long about that either and said, "Sure."

When they finished, he took a quick shower, got dressed, grabbed the duck back, and left. When he got out to the street, the duck was under his arm. It got spooked as a truck approached and jumped out from Dumb's grasp. It ran out into the street and was run over by the truck. The driver jumped out of the cab and saw what happened. He came over to Dumb and apologized. He felt terrible and said, "I am so sorry. I'll tell you what, here's $15 bucks to cover the cost of the duck." Dumb was confused but said, "You'll give me $15 bucks for the duck, I'll take it." He headed home, not sure what to tell his father.

That night the father called the three sons together and asked, "How did you guys make out?" Smart quickly responded and said proudly, "Dad, I got $2.50 for that duck."

Dad replied, "Nice. Not So Smart, how did you make out?"

Not So Smart responded, "Dad, I beat him. I got $5 for the duck.'

Dad was pleased and said, "Good for you. So Dumb, how did you make out?

Dumb was scratching his head and wasn't sure how to respond, but replied, "Well Dad, I'm not sure, but I think I won. I got a fuck for a duck, a duck for a fuck, and $15 for a fucked-up duck."

I have told that joke at least two hundred times over the last forty-five plus years. It never fails to get a hearty laugh from those listening. I apologize to both Lorraine and Teri, my wives, for also having to listen to it those two hundred times. Now, go ahead and laugh.

One confusing result of dating and then marrying Teri was that I completely stopped dressing as a female after I met her. I had been dressing a lot while still married to Lorraine, but I lost the desire when I found my new love. She was meeting all my feminine needs. She was sexy, beautiful, and a woman's woman. When we would go out on dates, I watched her process to get ready and putting on her makeup carefully. I was envious as up to that point I had never used makeup as part of dressing up. I was living my femininity through her. I did not miss dressing at all. I was concerned that someday she would find out and end our relationship. I would later find out in our relationship what kind of woman she really is. I went 10 years without even really thinking about dressing. I was so busy with my work career that I never gave it a second thought. I thought that I had beaten the addiction, but that would prove to not be the case.

Today, I often read social meeting posts from friends in the same situation that they are "stopping dressing for good." They purge all their clothes in the hopes that will help, but the reality is that it does not. It is an addiction that can be spurred on by assorted reasons like stress, strong sexual desires, or just seeing or touching sexy female attire.

In the mid-2000s, I found myself going back to dressing. I would wear Teri's lingerie and clothes while home alone. It was overly exciting for me. I often felt complete panic when I was dressed and heard her or someone coming home early or without notice, which did not happen very often. My usual modus operandi was to have her call me when she was leaving work so that I could change back to male-presenting clothes. I had started wearing make-up, which I would carefully put on and then make sure it was completely taken off.

I had a lot of guilt over dressing as I knew if caught it would be perceived as not only wrong, but very strange. But anyone fighting an addiction, like drugs or alcoholism, is fully aware that it can be difficult to stop. I was no different. I always wanted to stop and would go for brief periods without dressing, but then I would fall back into it.

Thanks to the internet I was reading and learning more about cross-dressing. I read that many men were dressing as women and that I was not alone. Like many, I would go for the sexy look with tight clothes, cleavage, and heavy makeup. I would spend hours looking in the mirror and marveled at my appearance as a woman. I had become a narcissist. It was confusing.

On a typical day, I would dress up and then go for car rides, not putting my wig on until I was safely in the clear. I loved how I looked and thought I could "pass," which was the goal. I remember the first time I drove to Salt Lake City to go shopping. I was a nervous wreck. It was obvious that I was a guy dressed as a girl, but I wanted to do it and could not care less what others thought. I started buying clothes at a rapid pace but kept them hidden from Teri. I was spending quite a bit of money, primarily at consignment shops. I kept this from Teri for many years without getting caught. I knew I was being deceitful, but I rationalized it by thinking it was not hurting her. I was so wrong. It was not until 2009 that I finally came clean and told her. I took the biggest chance of my life knowing full well it could end our marriage, but after asking lots of questions she said she understood and that I could continue dressing. I was also slowly becoming more feminine. I shaved my body hair, wore clear nail polish, dyed my hair, and was always tan. I felt happy and content and would stay that way until 2015 when Caitlyn Jenner introduced herself to the world and then my world would change dramatically. It was then that I decided I needed to find the underlying cause of what was going on.

I started seeing a gender therapist in Salt Lake City. At first, I was uncomfortable opening up to her as it was embarrassing and humbling. But I slowly felt at ease and out spilled my truths. I told her everything from when I was eight years-old to the present day. It was the beginning of lifting a huge burden off my shoulders. After months of telling her my story, she finally told me that she thought that, indeed, I was a transgender woman. I recall when I was first going to Diva Las Vegas in 2010 and meeting some transgender girls. I did not believe that I would ever be at a point that I would identify as transgender like them. I always thought that I would be a male who cross-dressed. In some ways it was a relief for me to hear the truth of who I had become. But when she asked me what I was going to do now that I had an official diagnosis, I was stumped. I came home and Teri and I had a long, heart to heart, life changing conversation. We agreed that it would be okay for me to be Cami and dress as often as I wanted. We planned a big house party on March 29, 2016, to tell all our local friends. It was an invitation-only affair with over thirty people on the guest list. Many thought we were announcing our divorce, but we shocked them even more by telling them I was a transgender woman. The support was amazing and although I did lose some close friends, most have accepted me to this day.

However, there was still one major issue that was preventing me from being a full-time transgender woman. I was still working as the executive director at Temple Har Shalom in Park City. I was hiding my big secret from the board, staff, and congregants. I worried that if I came out to them, I could be terminated, or congregants would resign if they thought that me transitioning would cost the Temple income. It was not until August of 2016 that after a series of fortunate things happened that I came out full-time. I was done cross dressing and could live my authentic life as a transgender woman.

Paying It Forward

One Saturday night in Vegas in 2017, myself and some trans friends were at the Paris Casino Hotel in a dance bar called Le Cabaret. I went to the ladies' rest room, which can always be interesting in Vegas. I walked into a stall and looked down to see a wad of bills laying there and upon counting it out, it came to $134. In an effort to find the owner, I left the stall and with a handful of women near the sink and in my best female voice, I asked "Did anyone lose some money." Well, all the women yelled, "I did." I quickly realized this strategy was not going to work, so I left with the money, thinking I would have to pay it forward somehow.

Later that night, I was with a close friend who wanted to gamble, which I do not ever do much of. I pulled out $20 from the wad of bills I had found. I was thinking that I would play with the found money. We played the roulette wheel and decided I would play whatever color, red or black, that had not come up on the roulette wheel in a while, since we could see the most recent spins on the electronic board. I picked black, put the $20 on it, and sure enough, it came up. My strategy, which is not really a strategy, worked six more times in a row and I was off and running. We had sat next to these guys who took a liking to us, especially this one guy who was sitting next to me. The problem was he could not win anything and was losing badly and quickly ran out of money. I thought to myself, "Here is a way to pay it forward," so I started giving him money to play with. Stacy, a good friend, also helped him by picking what numbers to bet. It took a while, and more money from me, but eventually he started to win and when I left, he was up quite a bit. I wound up with $152 in winnings in addition to what I won and felt good that I could help him out. So, I wound up with $286 from the weekend and only because I went, as I should, to the ladies' room and not the men's room.

Over the years, I have always been in decent shape, thanks in part to being continually active in sports, primarily skiing and golf. I can also say that walking our dog daily for 20 years has not hurt either.

It has been proven that dogs can be key factors in our health and well-being. Teri and I have been fortunate to have some awesome dogs during our relationship. We fell in love with English Springer Spaniels and have now had three, Dewey, Jake, and Jeter, the latter named after the famous Yankee, Derek Jeter. We have also had a border collie/collie mix named Chance, because we adopted him just before he was going to be put down, giving him that second "Chance." He was just a loveable, sweet dog. Teri and my first dog together was named Bruiser, a Springer Spaniel/Bernese mix, who we both adopted as ours upon my divorce.

In the absence of any children, which Teri and I consciously decided to not have, dogs have more than filled the void. We both have shared equally in taking care of them, but my role has primarily been to take them on morning walks, or should I say, they take me on morning walks. By some very rough calculations on my part, I estimate that over the years I have walked over 13,000 miles with these dogs, resulting in the burning of over 7,500,000 calories and the equivalent of walking two round trips from the east coast to the west coast. When I think about the benefits of all these miles, I recall the beautiful vistas, the diverse types of birds, horses, cows, deer and other animals that I saw.

The many paths I went took me to beautiful beaches, mountain tops, on national forest trails, through crackling electric pole line routes, river streams, and many cul-de-sacs. I saw beautiful homes, amazing landscapes, and snuck into many homes under construction. I have walked in temperatures as low as minus 15 and as high as the 100s through rain, snow, sleet, scorching sun, fog, and some of the best weather one could ever imagine. I have walked in New York, Martha's Vineyard, Florida, Vermont, Maine, and Utah. I never recall not wanting to take a morning walk.

Somehow, we always managed to have dogs addicted to a walk. They pestered me every morning with their begging eyes and constant whining. Once out the door, they would take off as if they had never been on a walk before. I am fortunate that they all were great off leash and I rarely had to keep them on one, until we adopted Charlie, our King Charles Cavalier, who I just could not trust to behave. With the others, if I said, "Come here," they did. We have had some encounters with other animals and dogs over the years, but none resulted in anything serious. I have only been warned by the local dog warden once to keep them on a leash. I read the laws and found out that with a shock collar and dog lead in your pocket, it was okay to let them run free. They love the freedom, and to some degree I did as well, as being pulled by a dog was not good for my back.

Over the years, I developed a reputation as the "dog walking, garbage picker," as I always pick up garbage that I see along the route. This was a result of my attending a self-improvement seminar called Life spring in 1991. One of the sessions centered on making a difference in the world by just picking one simple thing one could do daily to help save the environment. I chose as my lifelong personal vow to "always pick up and dispose of any garbage properly" that I see on the ground. I can honestly say that I never intentionally walk by garbage without picking it up if I see it. This has become my "one thing" to give back in life and is easily done on my morning walks. I cannot calculate how many pounds of recyclables or garbage I have picked up, but if I could, it would be a lot.

Dogs are a big part of our family. They have slept on our furniture, jumped on our laps, begged for our food, and followed us around the house constantly. They have had the run of the place but have been trained to stay on our property. Our house would not feel like a home without them greeting us upon our return, and the unconditional love they have for us. Whenever possible, they travel with us. They have been to many summer outdoor concerts, house parties, ruined many a game of croquet or bocce and been witness to many a shenanigan on my part.

We have had a couple big scares with their health over the years. A porcupine quilled one, and most have been chased by horses and skunked numerous times. Those were easy to deal with. In the winter of 2008, we decided to get a springer spaniel from an adoption center. We were thrilled and named him Jake, and we took him home after he received his shots. In the middle of the night, things got bad and quickly. We realized he was having an allergic reaction to the medicine and his throat was swelling up, causing breathing problems. We looked for some Benadryl in our house and found none. We called our good friend Lindsay, who had a young child, but she did not have any either. We called our vet, but they did not do any night calls. We were panicking, especially when we called a hotline which told us we had to go to the Alta hospital, which was open 24 hours. But the problem was that there was a raging snowstorm going on and Alta is an hour drive in clear weather. We loaded this little cutie, who was struggling for his life and headed for the hospital. The roads were terrible, but we did not have an option. I am a phone junky, but in the rush to get out of the house I left mine at home. We were shocked when suddenly, we heard Teri's phone ringing. It was in my coat for some strange reason. Teri answered, and it was our friend Lindsay. She had been checking other vets in the area and had found one local vet company called Park City Animal Clinic, owned and operated by Dr. Prior. He told Lindsay to tell us to come to his clinic in downtown Park City and he would meet us there. How fortuitous it was that she made the effort and that she called Teri's phone! We quickly made our way to his clinic only 10 minutes away and, sure enough, he showed up simultaneously. He immediately gave Jake a shot to reduce the swelling and after a few tense minutes, he started to breathe normally. He looked at us and said, "There is no way that dog would have made it to the hospital. It is a good thing your friend called me." An amazing turn of events sprinkled with some luck. We were so thankful, and Dr. Prior has been our vet ever since as we credited him for saving Jake's life. He also euthanized Jake when he succumbed to cancer in 2014, some nine years after he saved his life. We love that man.

While we lived on Martha's Vineyard, our other house, Jake was our dog. I will never forget when he was a puppy the first time, I taught him to swim in Lake Tashmoo, where we lived. He took to it like a fish and would love to swim and chase tennis balls that I threw in the water. He loved to roam the water while I tried to collect clams from the shallow water along the shore, often in front of Kenneth Cole's summer residence. The most fun was when on Saturday afternoons he and I would go to the lake and get in my kayak. I taught him how to ride with me and sit perfectly still. I would paddle us around all the power boats casually anchored or rafted together in the lake. Jake looked statuesque in his seat between my legs. He was a phenomenal chick magnet, and I was awarded free beers that would be offered by anyone who wanted to meet Jake and say hi. God, those were fun days on the Vineyard.

In 2016, we had another major scare, this time with Jeter. He loves his morning walk and is always sniffing for something or springing around, being a Springer Spaniel. Sure enough, he must have jumped on a broken bottle, which cut into the tendon area of his front paw. I quickly noticed the cut, thanks to the blood pouring out of him. Luckily, I was close to the house and Teri was a little late leaving for work. I ran back to the house and yelled for her to help me. We quickly loaded him into the back of one of our SUVs. She drove, as I held pressure on his cut to slow the bleeding. It was bad and I knew it and we arrived just as the clinic was opening for the day. The clinic staff and doctor jumped into action, and he was immediately taken into surgery where they were able to stitch him up, good as new. What a scare it was. It once again proved just how much we love our dogs and how much we will spend to keep them with us.

This past year, a friend and I travelled to Steamboat Springs to ski. On the way home, we stopped in Dinosaur, and she bought some chocolate edibles. After we got home, we went out and when we came back, she went up to her room to change. She came downstairs and had the package of edibles in her hand. She said, "Cami, eight of the ten edibles are gone." I immediately looked at Charlie, who was sitting at the front door in the sun. I called for him and he got up and awkwardly came towards me, walking almost sideways. We knew he was the culprit. He had gone into her room and somehow got into the package. I was truly scared he would die. We raced to the animal clinic with me holding him in my arms. He kept falling asleep and was unresponsive. It was scary. The animal clinic brought him right into the back to work on him. After an hour, the came out and confirmed that he was stoned, which I already knew. They told me to take him home, put him to sleep, keep an eye on him overnight, but he should be okay in the morning. Sure enough, the next day he woke up bright eyed and bushy tailed. It amazed me that he could have recovered after eight pieces. I have one and get an amazing buzz. Since then, he keeps asking for more, but we have cut him off from any marijuana.

I am a firm believer that dogs complete a home. They give so much for so little in return. Their unconditional love is so gratifying. As I sit here authoring this book my dogs, Charlie and Jeter, often have their heads resting on my leg, waiting patiently for a pat on the head. If only our lives were so easy.

The first 30 years of my life I lived in Poughkeepsie, New York. I lived in my parent's house for the first 22 years, and upon getting married to Lorraine, we moved to an apartment off South Road in Poughkeepsie. We bought our first home near my parents on Mockingbird Lane. I loved Poughkeepsie until we started going up to Vermont to ski at Killington. We loved Vermont, so we decided to buy a lot on Little Lake St. Catherine, about 50 minutes from Killington. We started building our second home in 1982 and moved there permanently in 1983 after I was hired by Killington Ski Resort.

We finished building the house enough to move in, although there was still a lot to do, including building out the second-floor bedrooms for the girls and a bathroom. We then bought the building lot next door and started building what we thought would be a spec house. We put it on the market as it was being built, and a couple from New York City saw the house and wanted to buy it, so we sold our house to them and moved into the spec house. It was a small house, but genuinely nice with a big deck. Unfortunately, I was commuting to Killington every day, which was taking an hour, and Lorraine was commuting to Rutland to the hospital, so we decided to build a house close to both our jobs and wound up in North Clarendon, Vermont.

Once I got separated, I moved into a condominium at Killington, one that my brother Jim and I both owned. It was nothing special, but it worked temporarily. Eventually I would start to date Teri and we moved in together in a townhouse in Mendon, Vermont. It was big enough to accommodate the kids when they would stay with me. I stayed there until I moved to New Hampshire in 1991 where I rented a large condominium in Woodstock.

In 1993, I accepted the job at Sunday River. Teri and I had gotten married, so we rented a large townhouse at the Powder Ridge project at Sunday River. It was close to the mountain and spacious. We stayed there until we bought our first house together on Songo Pond in the unincorporated town of Albany, Main. We loved this Cape Cod home and added a two-car garage and a huge family room off the back of the house with a large deck. We also bought a parcel of land across the street right on Songo Pond and refinished it into a small dock house and dock area. It was the quintessential lake house with an easy drive to Sunday River and Gould Academy where my daughter Lindsay went to high school.

In 1998, upon my transfer to Sugarbush, we bought another Cape Cod with enormous potential and great views of the mountains. It had an unfinished foundation designed for a two-car garage and whatever you wanted to build above it. We hired a friend, who was a contractor, and added a large new master bedroom with a fireplace above the garage and a large master bath. We also built a huge deck with a good portion being a screened in porch. It was beautiful, and we transformed an old home into a beautiful ski home overlooking Mt. Ellen (Sugarbush North) Ski Resort and Mad River Glen Ski Area.

We then bought the lot next door in the hopes of building a spec house, but the land did not perk, so we sat on it. We sold the property to my insurance agent, who somehow found a way to get the land to perk and ended up selling it for a huge gain. He eventually moved to Park City, and I saw him at the liquor store one day. He told me how much he made on the sale, and I was sick. The phrase, "Shoulda, woulda, coulda" certainly applied.

We moved to Martha's Vineyard in April 2000. At first, we lived in the Hanover House Bed and Breakfast in a two-room apartment with a kitchen that was also used to serve our guests. It was tight, and we were loving and living our job, so we looked for a house to get us out from being 24/7 at the inn. We found a cute 1790ish home that had been moved to the Vineyard from New Hampshire and then rebuilt. It was a cool house with a lot of character, but its ceilings were only seven feet tall, and the quarters were tight. It had the coolest green house that served as a family room/dining room with a beautiful wood burning fireplace. We had some intimate dinners in that house while we were there.

Being entrepreneurs, Teri and I had come upon and bought two four acre lots within easy walking distance of Lake Tashmoo. It was a beautiful, wooded area with a direct easement to Lake Tashmoo. We started building what we thought would be a spec house, but as it progressed, it became obvious that we loved what we were building and wanted to live in it. We sold our in-town house and moved into the Tashmoo house in 2004. It had an amazing back courtyard with terraced gardens loaded with hydrangeas and other beautiful plants.

I then brought in a partner, Steve Ellicott, a long-time friend, in a spec house project I wanted to build on the Vineyard, not too far from my new home. I was running the project and Steve was an investor. When finished, we put it up for sale, but it was listed just as the real estate market was dropping, so we sat on it for two years. We would do short term rentals as we did with our new home. When our new home was rented, which occurred often as it was a stunning home, we would move over to the spec house. We finally sold it, but lost money in doing so.

In 2000, a good friend at the time, Joe Eldridge, bought a beautiful 800-acre ranch in Kamas, Utah just outside Park City. It was called the High Star Ranch, but Joe changed the name to the Diamond J Ranch. Teri and I were hired to be hospitality managers for the ranch, which we would rent out to guests. It was a great gig and a fun place to work. We bought our now permanent home in Kamas in 2004 when the Ranch boss could not afford the new home he had just built. We swapped homes and he moved into the rent-free guest house, and we bought his house at a great price. We were very fortunate to have bought it when we did as our whole lives changed. It is still our permanent home and we have added additions to enlarge it and we just love it.

In 2003, Florida would become our new destiny. We had some good friends who also owned a B&B on the Vineyard near ours. They bought a second home in University Park Country Club in Sarasota, Florida. Teri's parents lived in Sun City, Florida, a 40-minute drive, so while visiting them we went to see our friends and fell in love with the community. We quickly found a cute fixer upper that we thought we could live in part-time, fix up, and flip for a profit. We should have never sold that house as we bought it at a decent price, and it was interesting with a cool courtyard in the middle. We met a nice couple who were neighbors and have remained friends. We owned it for about one year when it sold for a good profit.

We were hooked on flipping houses, so we found another to remodel and sell. It was a smaller home but had a nice pool and was on the golf course. We made a good profit again, so we bought another bigger, better home that did not require any renovation as it had just been renovated. We decided to live in this house while in Florida.

We lived in all these homes over the course of six years, and we would stay in all three homes we owned over the course of a year. We would be in Park City mid-December through March, then we would go to Sarasota for April and May before heading to Martha's Vineyard from June through September. The final leg was to Florida for Oct through mid-December. It was a great life, although we felt like nomads. We logged a lot of miles on the road. We drove for a couple reasons. First, we had two dogs that had to get to the new destination and second, we needed a second car at that location. When we were not occupying the place, we tried to rent it weekly. At each home we had great friends who we enjoyed seeing when we were there. It was always a new adventure and while we travelled the country, we still managed to run all our businesses at each location. It ended in 2010 when we were forced to "short sell" our Sarasota and Vineyard homes, resulting in us moving full-time to our Utah home.

It was a crazy experience for several years. Teri was always there by my side, through the good, the bad, and the ever changing. House flipping almost sunk us, but somehow, we managed to get through an exceedingly tough time and have fun along the way. It was quite the ride.

We have now been living in our Kamas, Utah home full-time since August 2008. It is only twelve miles from Park City with an easy drive into town on a four-lane highway with incredible views of the Timpanago Mountain range, as well as stunning views of the Deer Valley Ski Resort, Park City Mountain Resort and the Jordanelle Reservoir, a Utah State Park. We feel incredibly lucky to have purchased this home only one year after it was built. Over the years we have made numerous improvements, most notably adding a large sunken family room and a three-season room that we spend most of the summer enjoying. Over the past two Covid-19 years, I took the opportunity to build a new 20x10 foot vegetable garden. I tend to the garden with love and care as if the veggies were my children. However, the reality is that it would be far cheaper and easier for me to just buy our veggies from the farmers market in town, but why do that?

I have been a highly active and competitive golfer over the years. I started golfing when I was about seven years old. My father worked at IBM in Poughkeepsie, New York and we had memberships at the IBM Country Club, which was a leisurely walk from or house. I can even remember my membership number, which was 377500-03. There was an 18-hole golf course available to us at no cost, so when I had a chance to play, I was eager to do so. It was a fun, yet challenging course. The first hole was a steep downhill drive, which made you feel good with your opening shot because it was bound to result in your ball getting to the bottom, regardless of how good or bad the shot was. The hole also served as a sledding hill during the winter, and it was a blast. Today, it would be deemed too steep and dangerous, but those were different times, and for years we had the most amazing times.

Back in those early days, I was not a particularly good golfer as I was learning the sport, but when I became a firefighter, I started to play more often, and my handicap started to drop. We played courses all over Dutchess County, including McCann, Vassar, College Hill, and New York State courses. When I moved to Vermont, my game started to peak. I played three great courses often, one being Lake St. Catherine, the other Lake Bomoseen, where I watched Ted Williams playing once, and Killington, which was a new mountainous course, a true test of one's skills. I started playing in golf tournaments, such as the Leaf Peeper and the Ice Breaker at Lake St. Catherine and member-guest tournaments whenever asked. I loved the competition and did very well, especially playing with a great friend, Larry Wayne. We "bing, bonged" well and won quite a few tournaments and I believe our competitors knew they were in for a tough match when they faced us. Once, in a member-guest with Larry at Bomoseen Gold Club, I was set to tee off on the first hole with a crowd of onlookers watching. I was taking a practice swing when I inadvertently nipped the ball with it drippling off the tee towards those watching. The stroke had to count which hurt and so did the laughter from other competitors. Not a wonderful way to start a tournament, but that's golf.

Over the years my handicap has fluctuated, reaching as low as two, and then settling in around seven for many years and now, as I have aged and started hormones effecting my strength, stands at 10, also partially due to a torn rotator cuff that has impacted my swing. I have played some great courses over the years, including Spanish Bay in Carmel, California near Pebble Beach and where I shot a seventy-nine; Lahinch and Doonbeg in Ireland; Mid-Ocean in Bermuda; and Victory Ranch in my home state of Utah. The memories of these courses will long live with me.

I am proud to have won Club Championships at Killington Golf Club, Lake St. Catherine Golf Course, and the Park City Muni. I have won member-guests at numerous places, including Bethel Country Club in Maine with my best man Brian Ganey. Another highlight was to play in the amateur Ryder Cup in 1999, which was simply amazing and included having Bob Cousy as the guest speaker at the farewell dinner.

My competitive spirit typically involves betting on myself or my team and, over the years, I would venture to say that I have won more than I have lost. The reason is that, when under pressure, I play better than I normally would. My competitive juices start to flow when playing, but I would also say that most people enjoy playing with me because I can be fun to be with. As mentioned earlier, I do normally play barefoot, which always provokes questions from strangers. Being trans adds to the mystique and confuses most who do not know me. I still play from the men's tees, which might confuse some as they think if I am displaying my femininity, why not do as other women do? Well, the answer is simple. I do not want to cause conflict with women who might think it is not fair and, being the competitive player I am, the men's tees keep me challenged. Someday that may change, but for now, it is what it is.

I love golf, but I have always said that a day skiing is better than a day golfing as most ski days are usually more fun and rewarding than a day on the links, which is not always as fun as I would hope.

I am happy to say that Teri has become a golfer and is doing very well at the game. I look forward to when she retires, and we can play more together. She hits the ball very well and is consistent. She understands the game, the etiquette, and the rules, and is fun to play with.

So, what has my life been like over the past six years? Since transitioning full time in 2016, I have experienced much love and acceptance as well as continued rejection, but certainly less emotional pain. Why? Well, I am just a more confident trans woman. I have taken on an advocacy for the LGBTQ+ community that brings me the strength to move forward in a positive way, regardless of those that have not accepted me for who I want to be. I am still hopeful that Teri's family and mom will be willing to see me sooner rather than later and that some of the friends I have lost in transitioning would want to rebuild our friendship. Time will tell.

I felt that my public speaking skills could benefit my community and in 2019, upon finishing my first memoir, I began to develop what I refer to as a Cami Talk. This talk focuses on my experience in taking on risk to further one's life and accept the positives or negatives that result. I discuss the courage it takes to come out as transgender, especially for those who are younger and are seeking to live their authentic life. When one does things others cannot or will not do, that takes courage and that is often the case for those who come out as LGBTQ+.

I was fortunate to have been asked to do a TEDx Park City talk with a 16-year-old transgender male, Jace Deninger, in late 2019. The talk was moderated by a good friend, Bari Nan Rothchild, and included both of us telling our transition stories from the perspective of our ages, with me being sixty-seven at the time and Jace being sixteen. It was long, but to our surprise, the main Ted Talk platform picked it up for distribution globally. It is called "Transgender by Generations" and I believe it gives a remarkably interesting perspective from us both based on our ages and when we decided to transition.

I have been fortunate to continue to help the transgender community by being one of the lead organizers of Diva Las Vegas, a gathering of hundreds of trans individuals from all over the globe in Las Vegas every year. I get a lot of joy in helping "newbies" come down from their hotel room for the first time dressed as a woman or organizing events and get togethers for the attendees. Trans lives matter!

I have been asked to be on the boards of two great organizations, Transgender Education Advocates, where I serve as treasurer, and Encircle of Heber City, where I can contribute my wisdom from my years of varied experiences. Both are vital organizations that help our LGBTQ+ communities in the Wasatch Back of Utah.

In early 2021, I was asked to help organize an LGBTQ+ task force for Park City that I currently co-chair. With a mission to create, maintain, and enliven inclusivity in the local community, it is something that I am honored to be a part of developing. This group, along with the Park City Pride group, marched for the first time proudly down Main Street in Park City in the annual 4ᵗʰ of July parade in 2021, which was an experience and feeling I will cherish until I pass. Love was in the air and the crowd warmly welcomed us as we walked by, cheering loudly, and giving us a feeling of acceptance. I am so fortunate to live in the Park City community, where I am always warmly welcomed wherever I go. I am proudly the most visible trans woman in the area and I am often out dancing at local watering holes or concerts where I am visible to many. I am sure people look at me and have their opinions, but I do not care what they say or think. I am who I want to be.

In late 2021, a friend asked that I apply and then I was accepted into the Park City Leadership Class 28. This is a year-long development program to incubate future leaders of the Park City and local community. It was a true honor as there are only about thirty people invited each year. At the youthful age of sixty-eight, I started off on a self-help and development program. It is a serious commitment of time and effort, but I welcome the opportunity to be one of the first trans people in the program and second oldest in Class 28, the best class ever.

Up until the winter of 2021-22, I had worked as a greeter at the ticket booth at Canyons Village, which is part of Park City Mountain Resort. This position gave me an opportunity to be out in the public domain as a transgender woman. I thoroughly enjoyed meeting and helping guests and showing them that trans people are nothing to fear.

So, as you can see, I have been remarkably busy over the past few years. Since I am retired, I have had the time to devote to all these efforts. Advocacy can be like a real job, just without pay. I do it because I care about the LGBTQ+ community and helping others. I do it willingly and love every minute of it. I thoroughly enjoy giving my Cami Talks and will continue to do them if I am asked. In fact, I have been asked to be the guest speaker at the Helper City Pride event in Carbon County, Utah in June of 2022.

COVID was an interesting experience and time in the years since I transitioned. I had moments of concern, especially when Teri, who led the effort to set up testing sites around Park City, came down with COVID around Christmas 2020. It was a scary time, but I am happy to say she has had a full recovery. I have managed to get through it without getting it so far in its various forms. Pure luck. Although I have followed the rules as directed, I have been going to concerts, shows, sporting events, and living my life as normally as possible. I have managed to give several Cami Talks to various organizations and have continued my advocacy for the LGBTQ community especially during COVID.

I have also been, not busy, but taking my time to finish this memoir. Like a fine wine, memoirs take time to mature—and to gather all these experiences!

I have accomplished much since transitioning. I have been fortunate to build many great relationships that have replaced some that I lost. I can honestly say that I love my life right now. I feel I have reached the ultimate in self-actualization, which was one of my main goals. My life is full of love and kindness. I once had my pharmacist say to me after reading my first memoir,

"You know Cami, when you were Tom, I thought you were a bit of an asshole. Since your transition to Cami, you are such a different, kinder, and nicer person." Kind of a backhanded compliment, but likely the truth. I live my life to the fullest every day and I am often told on social media that I am, "Livin the Life." It is true, I am.

Speaking of social media, I must admit that I post a lot of my life on Facebook and Instagram. Why? Well, I believe most of my posts carry a thoughtful message, a nice picture of our adventures, and fun with family and friends. Since January 20th, 2021, I have not had a reason to post any political messages after Trump left office, which has been such a blessing.

I am blessed that my two daughters, Erin and Lindsay, and their families have accepted me without reservation. My grandchildren, Marisa, now thirteen, and Patrick, now eleven, have developed into great kids and I feel their love towards me. I am so fortunate to have them close to me so I can be part of their lives as they grow into mature adults. All of them love to ski and I love spending time on the slopes with them. It is a lifetime bond that brings us all boundless joy. Erin and Lindsay are doing very well in their careers, which makes me proud.

One constant in my life continues to be my amazing spouse of 29 years, Teri Cook. Many people often comment to me that the person with true courage and dedication is Teri. They are amazed that she would accept me as wholeheartedly as she has. She is truly my rock and there is virtually nothing that we do not share or ask for advice from each other. We love to travel and when we do it, it is fun to see how well we get along. She has an adventurous side and hates the felling of FOMO. In 2021, she stepped down from managing the Intermountain Park City Urgent Care Clinic into a registered nurse roll at the clinic. It has given her a lot more time off, less stress, and I have seen a dramatic change in her personality. We are headed off to Sicily in May of 2022 on a "bucket list" trip. Turns out that in her lineage she has a bit of Sicilian in her. I look forward to her retirement in a few years, which will give us the opportunity to travel even more then now.

I recently read an amazing book called, *Courage Is Calling*. Among many things it speaks about is that one should not be afraid of showing courage by taking risks in their lives. I completely subscribe to this logic and one of my Cami Talks is all about how people should not be afraid to take on risks as the rewards can be life changing. That is the case with me. I stepped out of my box and jumped in with both feet into a new world and love every minute of it. I hope you will take on more in your life and feel the potential accomplishments that are out there for you.

Finally, in the spring of 2021 my first wife, Lorraine Davies, passed away after an 11-year battle with a brain tumor. I have experienced death many times over the years, and it is never easy, but Lorraine's passing hit me hard. She was my first true love and the mother of my two amazing daughters, Erin, and Lindsay. She fought a courageous fight, and this book is dedicated to her.

Thanks for reading my book. I really appreciate it and hope you have enjoyed yourself. If you did, or not, please write a review on Amazon.

I love the LGBTQ community, and most especially the transgender community. However, just today, I am reading with deep concern about efforts by various state legislators to block trans kids from playing sports and receiving affirming health care treatment. In fact, the state of Idaho is proposing lifetime prison sentences for those helping trans people with affirming health care. Florida just passed legislation called, Don't Say Gay, which prohibits educators from saying anything to kids from kindergarten to third grade about the LGBTQ community. How could that be? Is this the America our forefathers imagined? What has gone wrong with our society that has pushed some this far that we are so hated, discriminated against, and denied our basic rights as citizens?

What can you do? Whether you are an advocate, an ally, part of the community, or simply someone who cares, please take the time to write or call your state legislators in opposition if you hear about a bill being proposed that would negatively affect the LGBTQ community.

I would also encourage you to listen to podcasts, interviews, or read articles about the LGBTQ community. If you Google Cami Richardson, the various podcasts and blogs that I have been part of, and stories written about me will pop up for you to hear or read. I believe you will find them helpful, especially if you or a loved one needs counsel.

I am always here to help, so I can be reached by writing me at camirichardson53@yahoo.com. If you or an organization your associated with would like me to speak either in person or virtually, just ask. I would be happy to do so.

Work History:

Paper carrier

Red Bull Motor Inn - Dish washer

Dutchess Golf Course - Golf caddy

Gas station attendant

Merit's Department Store:

> Cosmetics department sales
>
> Auto shop department sales
>
> Rug department sales

IBM Country Club - Athletic office attendant

IBM - Assembly line worker

AB Dick Company - Salesman

Arlington Fire District:

> Volunteer firefighter with Croft Corners Fire Company
>
> Paid firefighter
>
> Municipal training officer

William Dean Trucking- mover

Tax consulting business - Owner

Vassar College - Vending business co-owner

Hudson Valley Sports Productions - Producer

Vermont State Fire Service - Instructor

Wells, Vermont - Volunteer firefighter

Killington Ski Resort

> Internal auditor
>
> Lodging department controller

Pico Development Company - Controller

Pico Visions - Owner

Jiminy Visions - Owner

Killington Ski Resort - Manager of Operational Controls

Killington Ski Resort - Division Controller

Basketball official

Great Expectations Health Club - Part owner

Loon Mt. Ski Resort - Treasurer and Director of Base Operations

Sunday River Ski Resort - VP of Finance and Base Operations

American Ski Company - Sr. VP of Finance/Chief Financial Officer/Board member

Sugarbush Ski Resort - Managing Director

Tamarack Ski Resort - Consultant

Hanover House Bed and Breakfast- Owner

Heather Gardens Nursery - Owner

JET Construction/Development - Part owner

Fairwinds Affordable Housing Development

Modular Homes on MV- Developer/owner

Tisbury Fire Department - Volunteer firefighter

Lespri Property Management - Managing director

Beadniks Sarasota - Majority owner

Beadniks Park City - Owner

Summit County Beef - Executive director

Summit County Beef - Owner

Park City Local Card and Park City Mobile App Business - Owner

Park City Meat Company - Part owner

Temple Har Shalom - Executive director

Park City Mountain Resort - Greeter/ticket fulfillment

Canyons Golf Course - Player service representative

Ski Utah - Surveyor

Positions Held:

Our Lady of Lourdes – Student Council

Croft Corners Fire Company - Treasurer

AFD Local Union 2393 - President

Organized 1980 Winter Olympics Volunteer Fire Brigade

Organized Longest Day of Golf, Killington, VT. for the American Cancer Society

Wells Volunteer Fire Department - President

Junior Achievement of Rutland – Board of Directors

St. Michael's College, Vermont. - Advisory Board

Bethel Chamber of Commerce Golf Committee - Chairman

Redstone Merchant Association - President

Kimball Junction Business Association - President

Summit County Beef – Executive director

Transgender Education Advocates - Board member/treasurer

Heber City Encircle Home - Board member

Park City LGBTQ Task Force – Co-chair

Diva Las Vegas - Lead Organizer

Made in the USA
Columbia, SC
26 May 2022

60893635R00078